# THE CRAFT OF WRITING
# IN SOCIOLOGY

D1615703

MANCHESTER
1824

Manchester University Press

# THE CRAFT OF WRITING IN SOCIOLOGY

Developing the argument in undergraduate essays and dissertations

**ANDREW BALMER AND
ANNE MURCOTT**

Manchester University Press

The rights of Andrew Balmer and Anne Murcott to be identified as the authors of this work have been asserted by them in accordance with the Copyright, Designs and Patents Act 1988.

Published by Manchester University Press
Altrincham Street, Manchester M1 7JA
www.manchesteruniversitypress.co.uk

British Library Cataloguing-in-Publication Data
A catalogue record for this book is available from the British Library

ISBN 978 1 7849 9270 5 paperback

First published 2017

The publisher has no responsibility for the persistence or accuracy of URLs for any external or third-party internet websites referred to in this book, and does not guarantee that any content on such websites is, or will remain, accurate or appropriate.

Typeset by Out of House Publishing
Printed and bound by CPI Group (UK) Ltd, Croydon, CR0 4YY

# CONTENTS

# PREFACE AND ACKNOWLEDGEMENTS

The earliest antecedent for this book dates from 2001, when one of us (Anne Murcott) set up a writing group for PhD students and junior research fellows in the social sciences while holding a visiting position in New Zealand at CSAFE, University of Otago. On returning to the United Kingdom she then set up a similar group in Science & Technology Studies at IGBIS, University of Nottingham. This second group met monthly for close on a decade, attended at one time or another by something like thirty PhD students, of whom the other of us (Andrew Balmer) was one.

It is he who devised this book, created its shape and developed it especially for undergraduate students taking courses in sociology. Although our combined experience of teaching, supervision and management runs up to post-doctoral level, we have tailored the book towards undergraduate essays and dissertations in order to provide a solid grounding for developing basic techniques of writing, not simply to help students completing their first degree but also to provide a foundation for whatever direction they take after graduating. We are well aware that there are many books for students about how to write (and list a selection in the Appendix): advice about writing in general has a long, varied and often opinionated history, including 'classics' by Robert Graves, George Orwell and Margaret Atwood in the last hundred years alone. We have aimed this book at a very specific literal and metaphorical gap – the space beside the laptop during the very doing of an essay – in which it may sit ready to be consulted as the actual work of putting an essay together unfolds.

We are heavily indebted to fellow members of both original writing groups, but to the Nottingham one in particular for their commitment, colleagueship and great good humour – as well as for inventing the informal name of the group which we have impertinently purloined for the title of this book. We are also very grateful to undergraduate students who have given us permission to use extracts from their essays and dissertations to illustrate our discussion (and to whom we have randomly referred as 'she' or 'he' to help conceal their identity). We wish to thank everyone at Manchester University Press who helped us with this book, but especially Tom Dark, our editor, for his support and for extremely helpful discussions at critical stages of the book's preparation. Thanks are also due to the anonymous reviewers of the manuscript. And we would like to record our appreciation to many colleagues and friends for conversations about writing over as many years, including, in particular, Paul Atkinson, Wendy Bottero, Kate Bulpin, Hugh Campbell, Sara Delamont, Robert Dingwall, David Evans, Ian Jack, Hilly Janes, Lindy Sharpe and David Woodhead.

We alone, however, are responsible for errors or misconstructions in the final text.

# INTRODUCTION
# TO THE BOOK

The purpose of this book is to help you improve your writing, whether it is for essays, dissertations or exams. In turn, learning to write well should help you to get the most out of your university education as well as providing you with a set of skills that will stand you in good stead after you graduate. All this should also help you to enjoy writing, or, if you find it difficult and not so enjoyable, at least make it easier.

This book is for any student taking an undergraduate course in sociology in a UK university, or one based more or less on the UK university system including those in Australasia, Malaysia and the United States.[1] It is not just for those completing a degree in sociology, but also for students who are taking only a few or even just one sociology course or related courses. For those whose main studies lie outside of sociology, it will perhaps be especially useful if you are more accustomed to writing in psychology or other sciences and are now faced with writing sociologically. Our book aims to be readable and clear, written in as direct a style as possible to discuss matters that can be complex, in as practical a fashion as we can.

Time and again we have seen students struggle with some of the basics of writing. Yet such basics are rarely written down and taught in a practical fashion – the reason we have written this book. Indeed, the book is based on much of what we have learned with our students during discussions of their written work. Virtually everything we have included in the book has, at some point, somewhere, turned out to be useful to one or another group of students.

We think that clarity of both argument and style are the most important qualities to be found in your writing, not only now while you are still

---

[1] It means that throughout this book we also assume British English spelling and conventions for writing, which can vary considerably from those in Australia, the United States and elsewhere where English is a main language.

an undergraduate but for whatever you do when you graduate. It might be very pleasing if you could write to make people laugh or appreciate your literary turn of phrase, but you can still do very well in your studies without doing either. What you cannot do without is writing as clearly as possible and presenting your argument well.

There are many kinds of writing which you might be required to produce during your studies. For example, you might write essays, critical reviews, term papers, annotated bibliographies, essay plans, reports, blog posts and so on. Each of these forms of writing has its own specific, sometimes subtly different, qualities, some of which are shared and some of which are not. A blog post is not much like a report, for example, since the former adopts an informal style and generally aims to entertain, whereas the latter adopts a formal style and generally aims to summarise concisely the most important findings of an enquiry. We have focused this book on writing essays, for this is the primary form of writing which is required by sociological assessments. Moreover, essay writing requires you to construct an argument, draw together evidence and summarise key points, all of which are core skills that – if mastered – will allow you more easily to turn your hand to other forms of writing.

It will be helpful to see this book as a companion to writing your essays and other assessments. It is designed to be used alongside the actual work of reading and writing during your course, rather than read once and then put onto the bookshelf. Instead, it is a good idea to keep it on your desk or near to hand wherever you are working, so that you can return to it for reference as needed. Referring regularly to the book as you do your work can provide an opportunity to reflect not just on what you are writing (the content of your argument) but also on how you are doing it (the techniques which you are using to produce your argument and provide evidence for your points), so that you develop an appreciation of your own style, strengths and weaknesses and can consciously build upon them.

As we have written the book to support you in completing the assignments which you have been set as part of your education you will find that we have not included additional practice tests nor any exercises through which to work. Instead, we encourage you to experiment with the techniques and advice we review in this book in your non-assessed, formative assignments, and to do so regularly in order to learn them thoroughly for use in your assessed, summative assignments.

## THE CRAFT OF WRITING

The book is not called 'how to improve your essays' or 'how to write your dissertation' but 'the craft of writing'. To talk of craft may sound a bit old-fashioned or, worse, self-important. But we have used the term because of the way we think writing is best learned. In many ways, the craft of writing is learned by a novice in a similar fashion to learning to make a pot in a studio: creating something subtly unique, learning from a teacher through watching and listening. The process is almost the opposite of producing a standardised product in factories. Cars made on an assembly line, for example, are each identical to the next and all have to measure up to some prescribed set of specifications. Writing is not an industrialised process but a craft practice. Whilst you are at university to study sociology (or a subject closely related to it) you have also become a student of the craft of writing. In order to progress through your studies and to make the most of your time at university, and indeed the most of this book, it is worth thinking of yourself as a novice writer as much as a novice sociologist. Learning to write better is one of the most important things you can do with your time as a student for it will remain with you for the rest of your career.

Writing and reading are inextricably linked elements of the craft. The point of writing anything is to make it available for reading; even secret codes are meant to be read by someone. Improving your own writing will be greatly improved if you read widely and, as you do so, think about the way authors have crafted the books and articles you study. Reading and reflecting on how you read is integral to continuing to develop the craft of writing. On this note, it is primarily for convenience that we have organised the majority of the first part of this book according to what, at first sight, is the sequence of an essay: starting with reading and making notes, then exploring how to construct an argument based on your understandings of and critical reflections on these readings, before journeying through the construction of the beginning, middle and end of the essay, and concluding with the process of redrafting, editing and proof-reading.

In practice, however, this sequence commonly comes apart, with a good deal of doubling back along what initially seems like a logical, linear chain of events. In any case, thinking too rigidly in terms of this sequence risks reinforcing the idea that writing does not happen until very near the end of the process. On the contrary, writing starts – or should start – almost as soon as you first read the essay title. After all, looking at the title is bound to prompt some thoughts. It will do no harm and could end up being very useful to make a note of those thoughts right away. One thing on which we lay considerable stress is that you should be writing much of the time, at the very least a couple of pages once a week. As the American sociologist C. Wright Mills observed:

> You cannot 'keep your hand in' if you do not write something at least every week. (1959: 197)

> You will have to acquire the habit of taking a large volume of notes from any worth-while book you read – although, I have to say, *you may get better work out of yourself when you read really bad books.* (1959: 199; emphasis added)

As Mills obviously assumes, reading academic articles and books does not mean accepting what they have to say or copying the ways in which they have said it. When you read academic sociological work you will find that you agree with some of the arguments and disagree with others. This is an important part of *critical* reading because it opens up routes to crafting your own arguments. You will also find that some sociological writing is pleasing to read, but some is turgid or incomprehensible. This could be because the argument is opaque and difficult to understand, but it could just as well be that the work is badly written. Keeping this in mind as you read is important in developing your own writing.

On the face of it, critical reading is the beginning and writing the end of producing an essay – but only on the face of it. Academic reading should almost always involve writing. Even before deciding to make notes on something, a written record of the full bibliographic details needs to be made for future reference – and stored in the appropriate place, whether you choose to use bibliographic software such as Endnote or Reference Manager, or a plain Word document. And in creating this important record, it is often very useful to add a note to yourself in the process – maybe a reminder that this is an article that outlines an important concept for your essay or that the book has only one chapter to which you will want to return. Even such easy, quick remarks at a very early stage may be valuable as the work unfolds and may even find their way into the final essay itself.

As we have implied so far, writing has various uses. It helps create a record of something without having to memorise it. Making notes in a lecture helps remind you of what was covered and where it all fits into the course syllabus. Not only are your notes a record for future reference, the very act of writing them during the lecture can help you remember what was said. Writing is also extremely useful for working out what you are thinking or helping weigh up the pros and cons to help you to decide what you think of a debate. For all three of these uses of writing, you are the reader. You are your own audience, writing for yourself.

The writing which comes at the end of producing the essay is writing for a different audience, when the reader switches from being you to being your tutor or supervisor. By then, all the writing for yourself must be complete. You will, with luck, have kept the list of complete references in the right place, brought together what you need from your lecture notes that is relevant and, above all, have assembled the relevant parts of the notes you made on all you have read. With all those to hand, you will be able to arrange them into written plans for what you want to say in your essay, before going on to prepare a first draft, which, by the end, will have helped you to sort out more clearly and decisively what you think and the kind of argument you want to present. At this point it is time to redraft the essay and finally to write it for your ultimate audience – your tutor or dissertation examiners.

In just the same way that writing has various uses, so too does reading. There are obviously different types of academic reading, ranging from general background reading, studying textbooks, reading as a basis for a tutorial or class discussion as well as the reading dedicated to preparing an essay or a dissertation's literature review. Equally, in just the same way that academic reading should always involve writing, so writing should always involve reading. Reading through what you have just written is the only way of checking that it makes sense and that you have put down what you wanted. This will also help to reduce the number of times you write something you did not mean and to avoid repeating yourself.

## THE VALUE TO SOCIOLOGY STUDENTS OF LEARNING ABOUT WRITING

Just possibly, what distinguishes academic reading and writing from many other types of either activity is the importance of pairing reading and writing so that each repeatedly informs the other. Yet writing is a transferable skill which is bound to be useful after you graduate, no matter what you do in your work or leisure time. It is not merely a set of techniques useful for writing good essays and passing exams. It is a fundamental and enduring way of communicating. The written word is unlikely to become obsolete, even if all kinds of as yet unimagined means of communication are invented. Indeed, the American cognitive scientist, Steven Pinker, claims that 'more than ever before, the currency of our social and cultural lives is the written word' (Pinker, 2014: 8). It is often claimed in sociological circles that, in the West, we live in a communication or media culture due to a proliferation in recent decades of communication technologies and social media. Whatever the effects may be on the way we read and write, it is highly likely that reading critically and writing clearly will be at least as valuable in twenty years' time as they are now, if not more. Developing methods of learning to read and write more effectively needs to be taken seriously – something you should truly value. Do not, then, be shy about telling future employers, for example, that sociology – like history or philosophy – is a discipline in which the skills of learning to write and to read critically are honed and prized.

In the meantime, writing is the main way you will demonstrate that you have successfully grasped what is needed to be awarded your degree. Remembering who you are writing for at which stage, and why, will be invaluable when ensuring that you do not fall into the common trap of thinking that because (presumably) your tutor or examiner knows the material you are presenting, you do not need to spell things out. The reverse is the case. Reflecting on why your tutors are the readers will remind you that although they already know the material, their task is to check how well *you* know it. The sooner they can breathe a sigh of relief on discovering that you have shown that you know it well and have marshalled your points appropriately to support a carefully thought-through argument clearly and coherently, the happier they will be with your work.

Despite its being one of the social sciences, writing in sociology is more like writing in the arts and humanities than in the life and natural sciences. Although undergraduates taking sociology courses are not writing novels or journalism, they are studying a discipline in which the style is literary – more like a book, less like a set of notes, bullet points or list of procedures. For instance, the natural or life sciences are liable to require using the passive voice – 'an experiment was designed to control three variables' not 'I designed an experiment to control three variables'. In sociology it is common to write in the first person – 'I conducted ten open-ended interviews'. This might imply that the distinction is to do with methods. It is true that the image of a discipline such as physics is that it uses numerical data whereas an image of sociology is that it uses textual data, but this does not reflect the reality in either subject. Both natural and social scientists use qualitative and quantitative data to varying degrees and with sometimes different purposes. Sociologists must learn to write about both. Writing sociology essays requires you not only to cope with these different forms of data and to understand to some degree the techniques of their collection and analysis, but also to discuss debates, different theories or contrasting methodologies and to develop arguments. You need to deploy these skills together to address the essay title.

## FINDING YOUR WAY ROUND THE BOOK

We have written the book so that it can be used in more than one way. First we would suggest you read it all the way through. That will give you a good idea of where to find what you will need to look at again. Part I is organised according to stages of the essay-writing process, which should mean you can easily return to particular chapters to help you whilst you are working on an essay without having to read through the whole book again. Part II then deals with common issues experienced or questions that students ask about essay writing which do not directly relate to a particular section of an essay. Finally, Part III introduces some of the basics of grammar to help you to write good sentences and to use punctuation appropriately. Certainly you can easily find whole books on grammar. But we have included some material at the end for the convenience of having everything you may need to hand in just one book. We have pitched the level at which we present grammar, spelling and punctuation at that which our own work with undergraduates indicates is best suited to their essay and dissertation writing in sociology. Our selection of problems for detailed attention is based on the range of problems our students have trouble with.

So, whether you are someone who relishes essay writing or can find it a little daunting, this book is intended to be useful and to be used. If you are just beginning your studies in sociology, beginning with 'Beginnings' (Chapter 3) along with 'Reading critically' (Chapter 1) could be most useful to start with. If you have been studying sociology for longer, then focusing on 'Making an argument' (Chapter 2) and 'Making use of feedback' (Chapter 14) could be particularly useful. For in much the same way that essays do not get written in a linear fashion, beginning to end, a book that aims to help you write them will be most useful, after a swift skim through to learn what is on offer, when you pick out the most relevant sections for the essay you are currently working on. To help you to pick out the most relevant sections, we have included very brief summaries of the key topics covered at the end of each chapter in Part I. These can also be used as a reminder of the main things you need to be doing or to bear in mind when you are writing essays. Come back to these section summaries regularly, whenever you are required to write a piece, to point you towards the key parts of the book which might assist you with whatever it is you are currently writing.

# ✢ Part I ✢

# PRINCIPLES AND PRACTICES OF WRITING AND ARGUMENTATION

# ☙ 1 ❧

# READING CRITICALLY
# AND MAKING NOTES

It is no accident that the somewhat old-fashioned expression in the English language for studying a subject at university is 'reading'. In preparing your own texts for your degree course you will need to show that you have read relevant material. So you will have to incorporate into your written work reference to, and discussion of, the materials you have read. Although the requirement to cite, reference and organise your reading is most important in an essay, it is also necessary, albeit to a lesser degree, if you wish to do well in your exams. In both cases you have to weave texts (whether books, journal articles or chapters in edited collections) that you have read into your discussion to try to draw these materials together and compare and contrast them.

To be able to do this it is essential to read not only widely but also in depth, in addition to making useful notes on what you have read. Indeed, this is what constitutes much of the work of writing an essay. So the more value you place on the process of reading and making notes, the more your written work will benefit. Moreover, it is especially important that you read 'critically' in order to generate good notes that will help you to build the framework for your argument and enable you to shape your essays into a logical and concise structure. Here, incidentally, as elsewhere in the book, we use 'critical' in its scholarly sense. This involves being enquiring and open-minded and avoiding taking what you read at face value, all of which has to be coupled with dealing with concepts and using your skills of discussion and evaluation. Remember that this is different from the everyday use of the word 'critical' to mean being disapproving, derogatory or finding fault.

You may already have realised that in the type of focus on concepts and evaluation needed for academic work, it is important to have some sense both of what you are looking for as you read and of how to keep track of this information in your notes. In what follows we examine the key dimensions of critical reading and note taking. First of all, we look at how you can ensure you read widely, at the same time as maintaining a focus both on your topic area and on good-quality materials.

## HOW TO READ WIDELY

To read widely start with the basic reading required for your course. For most modules you will be assigned readings for your lectures and seminars. It is wise to read these as the course progresses and to keep your notes on them all together so that when the module ends you will have an organised collection of notes to get you going. However, you should make new sets of notes when preparing an essay to reflect what you have learned since you made the first notes on what you read. Essays normally focus on a particular part of the module and so it is a good idea to go over in depth the readings that were required for the lectures, seminars and workshops that covered the topic identified by the essay. An important element in understanding materials specific to the essay topic is to position them in the context of the issues dealt with in the course as a whole. So, for instance, imagine you are taking a course on 'Race and Ethnicity' and you are writing an essay on 'Whiteness and Class'. Focusing on readings around whiteness and class will be important, but equally important will be understanding how those readings and this issue fit into the broader cluster of issues, questions, theories and developments in the field of race and ethnicity studies in general.

Lecturers tend to choose the key readings for a course from the major thinkers on a topic, or to select articles and chapters that include good reviews of the material in that area. The latter in particular often include references to other important books and articles in the specific field. So, to begin reading more widely, look at the bibliographies of the required readings and pick out those that seem to be most relevant to the essay question you are tackling. Reading the abstracts of articles or the introductions and conclusions of books can be a good and quite quick way to get a sense of whether the work will be relevant.

When you go through your lecture notes and the key readings for a module, you can often spot who the key contemporary thinkers are in the particular topic area you are studying – quite simply, their names keep cropping up. So make a quick list of the names of the main scholars in the field and then look for these in a search engine. Because academics are increasingly required to make their materials publicly available, there are now good repositories of articles and other materials easily available on university and academics' personal websites. You can often find a personal or professional website for living academics on which they will have a list of their publications, sometimes highlighting their major outputs, often with a link to a free copy of an article. Reading additional material by key authors can be a good way to build your understanding of the topics and the context of the way their thinking has developed. Indeed, situating a specific book or article by one or another author in the broader body of their research and interests is often valuable for helping understand the significance of the specific piece with which you started – and it can be an effective way of opening your essay and getting to grips with its argument.

The amount of any one item you should read varies. Much of the time you will need to read the whole of a journal article, usually at least twice, to be sure you have grasped its import and to make critical notes. Now and then you may need only to skim an article or read one section. Similarly, you will sometimes need to read a book from cover to cover. Often, however, you can select chapters or sections that are most relevant – remember to check the index as well as the contents page to give you an idea of which sections to read. If you are not sure whether to read the whole text or just a selection, ask your tutors' advice. Listen out for the criteria they use to make the decision and, if necessary, ask them what those criteria are. That way you can gradually learn to make such decisions for yourself.

As you progress through this initial, focused process of collecting materials, be sure to read and make notes at each stage. And keep re-reading those notes, thinking about which, if any, have some sort of link with others and which do not. This will help you plan and shape your continued search for relevant reading, as well as helping you decide when you have enough to go on. It also means that you can develop and extend your notes in relation to each other while you work, rather than simply collecting a haphazard bunch of materials whose relations to one another have not been considered, which risks leaving you simply feeling swamped with no idea where to start.

Once you have done this initial reading you will probably have a good sense of the central concepts and themes about the topic you are studying. These should then form the search criteria you use in internet and library search engines. Starting from course materials and working outwards towards online searches is a good way of going about things because it helps you to shape your searches in a constructive and focused way. It gives you clear lines of enquiry and leaves you with a good sense that you are making headway. There is so much material online and in libraries today that it is very easy to get lost in it all. By drawing together recommended materials first and then using these as the basis for your wider searches you will save time and greatly reduce the risk of losing focus. Use your library's search engine, which will often allow you to find materials it holds both in hard copy and in digital form.

Be careful as you begin and progress through your reading not to fall into either of two traps. One trap to avoid is the possibility that an author may not be dedicated to the type of systematic study that is essential to academic work. Instead, an author may be presenting a particular 'line' or mounting a campaign, or may have a vested interest in putting forward some particular account. It is crucial not to rely on just one text to summarise a field or some other body of work. It is also crucial to refer back wherever possible to the original sources so as to check for yourself how those earlier works are being presented. The other trap is forgetting that some (often older) books, even in sociology, are written in a style that assumes consensus, or assumes that there is a single truth to be revealed and that the given text has discovered it. Such consensus less and less frequently holds and you should remember to read the 'voice' of a text as just one possible position on the subject, against which you might compare and contrast other voices, including your own. A helpful tip for spotting this kind of 'bias' is to check whether the author has adequately presented alternative viewpoints and made an argument in reference to other scholarship. Failure to do so can indicate that a view is being presented as fact.

## SUMMARISING AND LOCATING THE TEXT

When reading a text and using it in your essay it is very helpful to be able to quickly summarise and locate that particular text in its scholarly context.

### Summarising the text

Some texts that you will deal with in an essay form the primary focus or source through which you will develop your argument, so they will need additional, special attention. In order to summarise a text such as this you should identify its main argument. Think about what its main subject matter is and then break it down into a series of more specific claims. So, for example, we might say that Goffman's book *The Presentation of Self in Everyday Life* is concerned primarily with the way people manage face-to-face interaction in given situations. To add to this basic kind of summary it can be useful to reflect on a number of elements that most texts have, and how they are related. In short, you could consider how the methods, main arguments, theories and data are related. Looking out for these connections and mapping them out in relation to your major sources for your essays can be a useful way of organising some of your critical reading and note taking. You should also be looking for the evidence used to justify the arguments made in a text.

Try answering some of the following questions about the main texts that you deal with in your essays.

1. At what level of social organisation does the text conduct its analysis? Some examples could include:
   a. Macro structures such as social institutions, e.g. family and kinship, religion or education;
   b. Micro structures, e.g. social interaction, or forms of relationship, e.g. studies of friends, colleagues or acquaintances.
2. How do the methods and methodology relate to this level of social organisation? We can break this broad question down into two separate questions:
   a. Which method has been used for the study and what kinds of social phenomena can be studied using this method? For example, a social survey is most appropriate to enquire about patterns in society at the level of macro structures, as is the case with statistical analyses of social class.
   b. How does the methodology relate to the question posed by the text? For example, such a statistical examination of class is liable to assume a positivist methodological outlook and so will highlight concerns of validity, reliability and generalisability.
3. Is it a largely empirical or a theoretical work? If it is both, how are data and theory related to one another?
   a. Where do the data come from and what form do they take?
   b. How well do the data support the conclusions?
   c. Are there possible interpretations of the data which have been overlooked?

d. Are the theories developed based on the data?
e. Are new theories being justified on the basis of the data?
f. Are existing theories being used to interpret the data?
g. Would other possible theories have been more useful to inter-pret these data?
h. Is there more than one theory at stake?

By answering some of these questions you can begin to categorise the texts you are using in a more substantial manner and thereby make them more pertinent to a particular question. For example, exploring these questions in the case of Goffman's book, *The Presentation of Self in Everyday Life*, we might summarise it thus:

> The book is concerned primarily with how people manage face-to-face interaction in given situations, which is explored through what Goffman terms the 'dramaturgical method'. By invoking dramaturgy he draws a comparison between everyday life and the theatre. He uses this approach to explore the microstructures of everyday interaction, both those he observes in a range of situations first-hand and picked up from other sources. Based on these data of everyday life Goffman proposes a theory of social interaction as being made up of strategically managed performances.

By summarising the texts according to the way their methods, main arguments, theories and data are related, you can write concise state-ments about the way a given text could be useful to respond to the question you are tackling. For example, if you had to answer a ques-tion about gender you could relate Goffman's book to this topic by highlighting the way in which his dramaturgical analogy can be used to cast gender as a performance, the presentation of self, conducted in specific social situations as part of a strategic interaction between actors. In other words, answering some of these questions in your sum-maries allows you to point to the value of the text in approaching the question and can in turn lead your reader in the direction that your essays indicate. Indeed, summarising texts can often be a good way to begin essays (see Chapter 3).

Moreover, drawing out such relations between the various features of a sociological text can be a valuable way of learning how to compare the works of different thinkers. Comparing (and contrasting) texts is a good way of developing your ability to think critically. For example, looking at these features you might discern that a difference in argument between two thinkers perhaps arises as a consequence of their using different methods to approach the subject or comes about because they draw on data from different types of source. This illustrates a type of good, critical point to make and will allow you to articulate how different arguments have been developed by other thinkers and thus help you build your own argument alongside theirs by virtue of your pointing out those differences. We will consider these kinds of critical approaches to argument later in this chapter and in the following chapters.

## Locating the text

When summarising a book, chapter or article, it can be useful to 'locate' the text in its broader context. One of the several possible contexts for a text is important: all these materials share the context of the author's other works. In other words, you could ask yourself how – or whether – this particular book or article fits into their larger project of academic research. Looking over the author's body of work can give you a sense of where the key text with which you are dealing is positioned. Is this a foundational text from early in their career, or is it something more recent that depends on these earlier investigations? Is this a significant change in direction or turn in their work, developing a new way of looking, or does it extend and refine earlier positions? Answering these questions helps to set out the sense of the book as part of the history of an author's scholarly output.

In addition, we can locate a particular author's text(s) within a broader context of academic scholarship. Academics tend to work within a specific field of research, for example in the area of gender and sexuality, or ethnicity and race, and develop a line of argument and sets of data that are broadened and deepened over time. This work is often articulated in dialogue with other scholars and theorists. Indeed, an author frequently chooses existing approaches against which to distinguish their own work, or as a basis from which to begin their own contributions to the field. Understanding the context of an author's works can also come from looking at the time period and historical context in which the ideas were developed. You can ask what concepts, methods and materials were available to the author at the time, and how were they influenced by specific trajectories and approaches that were popular in the period. So paying careful attention to the date of what you are reading is very important – as is spotting whether there has been more than one edition, with the author having made considerable revisions since the work was first published.

In each of these contexts, of the author's other work and the broader academic field, we can also reflect on the more general importance for sociology of the questions with which these texts deal. What is it they are trying to accomplish from a broader sociological perspective? Are they even succeeding in doing so? Commonly, central academic texts in a given area of enquiry attempt to pursue some new way of thinking about or of studying a subject as a way of improving on earlier work and advancing the field. This might involve developing a new theory, be it of social order, interaction, identity, subjectivity, or action. Or it could be about advancing a fresh or more refined methodological approach to the study of social life. Think about how the material is presented in your lectures and keep these questions in mind when reading, for this will help you briefly summarise what it is that the authors of key texts are trying to accomplish.

Here is an example from a first-year sociology student essay in which the student explores the relationship between Comte and Durkheim. The student begins their essay by locating and contextualising these authors' work:

> It is important to examine the impact that Auguste Comte had on Durkheim's work. Comte was the first person to use the term 'sociology' and his main aim was to create a naturalistic science of society (Coser 1971). Comte is most famous for the development of positivism and the epistemology he developed had a substantial influence on Durkheim's work which followed (Morrison 2006). Comte described his methodology as 'reasoning and observation, duly combined.' (Coser 1971:3) He believed that in order to study society, social phenomena must be witnessed and observed whilst using objective rationality. This would lead to reliable theories being developed about society. Durkheim was particularly influenced by this positivist attitude towards studying society as well as Comte's philosophical concept of social realism, the idea that society should be studied independently of the individual. [Quotation from a first-year sociology student's essay]

In the extract above you can see how the student relates Durkheim's work to the context in which it was developed, namely against the background of Comte's development of positivism and social realism. This is a good conceptual introduction to Durkheim's work for it locates his ideas against the backdrop of work that Comte had already developed. By drawing attention to the connections between their work at the level of epistemology and methodology, the student clearly shows that there is a trajectory of thinking that helped to shape Durkheim's ideas. This can be a useful context later in the essay, to show, for example, how Durkheim developed novel contributions and how his work moved away from, but also arguably improved on, existing scholarship, at the same time as illustrating the way that his research, theories and interpretations were influenced by the period in which he was writing and by the wider debates current at the time. This can open doors to exploring the significance of different concepts and evaluating their usefulness. Understanding the context in which an idea was made use of and the background against which it was developed is an important resource for forming your own arguments.

## IDENTIFYING OBJECTS AND CONCEPTS

It is important that when you read materials for your essays and exams, you read critically in order to collect productive notes for making your argument. As we will describe later, an essay *is* an argument and so it is important to think in terms of potential 'lines of argument' when you are making your notes. A line of argument is built by use of 'objects', 'concepts' and 'propositions'. This is true of both social theory and empirical research, although the way in which objects are studied, concepts are developed and how exactly they are linked together varies between them.

Objects are those things that sociologists and other academics study. The way in which they define and study objects varies according to their research interests and disciplinary training. Much like a life scientist, chemist or physicist might write about cells, catalysts or quasars, sociologists too are concerned to write about the objects that interest them. Herbert Blumer, working in the tradition of symbolic interactionism, had this to say about sociological objects:

> We are accustomed perhaps to think of 'objects' as the hard and physical things in our world, such as a table, a hammer, a building, and the like. Mead uses the term in a broader sense to mean anything that

can be referred to or designated – a chair, a house, a horse, a woman, a soldier, a friend, a university, a law, a war, a meeting, a debate, a ghost, a task, a problem, a vacuum, and abstract things such as liberty, charity, intelligence, and stupidity. In this legitimate sense of being anything that can be designated or referred to, objects may be material or immaterial, real or imaginary; may be placed in the outer world or, as in the case of a sensation or a pain, lodged inside the body; and may have the character of an enduring substance such as a mountain or be a passing event such as a kiss. (Blumer, 2004: 39)

This range of objects that can be examined from a sociological perspective is part of what makes it such an appealing and potent discipline. It also represents a challenge for sociological writing, since such objects can be understood in a variety of ways. As a consequence, it can also be a challenge for students of sociology to identify the objects with which academic writing is concerned and it can be difficult to discern exactly how sociologists have defined their objects.

Similarly, there are a great many different sociological concepts that are used to describe objects from the level of everyday interactions between individuals to structural phenomena that span the globe, from agency to society itself. In addition, the meaning of the term 'concept' in qualitative research is different from its meaning in quantitative studies. Most books and articles neither specify nor explore how they will use 'concepts', instead assuming that what constitutes the function of the concepts will become apparent or is already a given by virtue of the methodological approach being adopted. To complicate things further, the word 'concept' is used in everyday conversation to mean something much more casual, such as a thought that has just occurred to someone, or an idea people tend to talk about. Even when not defining them, academic sociologists use concepts to mean something more precise and definite.

This book is not the place in which to get bogged down in a long-standing and complex debate about the nature of sociological objects and their relationship to concepts. Rather, our purpose here is to work out how best to make use of definitions of objects and concepts when they can be found in the academic literature, and what to do when such definitions elude you. We shall deal with the latter problem first.

At first sight, struggling to find how a particular object or concept has been defined in an academic paper might present quite a challenge. The most immediate action to take in this case is to read further. Often, academics fail to define their objects of interest or the concepts that they use because it is assumed that since readers are familiar with the broader academic literature, they will be able to discern this for themselves. It might also be because the academic has failed to think carefully about these issues. Your job, in conducting a critical reading of the literature, is to try to discern which of these is the case. You should begin by reading further materials, particularly those articles and books which are foundational texts in the field or which have marked a significant change in sociological understanding of a given topic, in order to find whether there are good definitions that you can use. If you cannot locate a definition then this itself could form part of your analysis. You might argue, for example, that the literature fails adequately to define the concept with which your essay is concerned. Of course, you can only do so confidently if you have adequately reviewed the academic materials. You might also explore whether definitions of those objects or concepts is implied in the material you have read, even if they are not explicitly stated. In order to make such an argument you will have to be able examine the way in which academics link together objects, concepts and propositions, which we further explore in the following sections.

Whilst they can be elusive, you will often find that your critical reading presents you with a number of definitions of objects and concepts that you can use to build your own argument. In the following quotation from David Morgan (2009) you should be able to see how he clearly sets out a definition of 'intimacy', a concept which he goes on to use in relation to the primary object of interest in his book, 'acquaintances'.

It is possible to see intimacy as consisting of at least three different dimensions, which do not necessarily co-exist in all interpersonal relationships. The first is physical or embodied intimacy. It is important to stress that this is not simply a question of the physical expression of sexuality. It also includes the physical aspects of caring or tending and those physical signs (holding hands or touching in particular kinds of ways) that demonstrate that some kind of interpersonal bond exists between the two people involved … Second, there is emotional intimacy, itself a complex and compound dimension. Thus it can include the sharing of deep feelings, anxieties, doubts and passions. But it can also include the recognition of the emotional needs or likely emotional responses of others, perhaps even at a non verbal level … Third, there is intimate knowledge. Intimates have particular knowledge of each other, knowledge which is conventionally denied to others outside this core of intimacy ... These three dimensions, taken together, pick up most of what is generally understood by the term 'intimacy' and define the characteristics of relationships defined as 'intimate'. (Morgan, 2009: 2)

Morgan gradually builds a picture of the concept of intimacy by outlining the three elements he considers to be important to its definition. Appearing early in the book, this definition serves to frame how the book will use the concept of intimacy in order to understand acquaintanceship in everyday life. In your critical reading of Morgan's argument, it would be important to pay attention to how this definition of intimacy is used to understand acquaintanceship in the remainder of the book.

Whether you are examining a theoretical or empirical text, it is important to understand how authors define their concepts as this can often be a source of conflict, disagreement or tension between different authors or academic traditions. One source of such conflict can be related to the use of different methods and methodological traditions. The academic debate in sociology regarding the use of concepts in relation to qualitative, quantitative and mixed methods has a long history and is likely to be the subject of at least some of your university courses. We will not rehash these debates here but mention of it should encourage you to pay similar attention to how concepts are being used in relation to particular methods as you get on with your reading in sociology. Ask yourself which concepts are being applied to which objects, whether these have been adequately defined and whether the connections have been well evidenced. Does the use of these concepts in these ways fit into a broader tradition in sociology? Examine whether the definition of the objects studied and concepts employed have been linked to the methodology being used in the research. Asking about or even challenging how authors have defined, used or refined concepts in these ways might form an important part of your own critical argument, which we will explore further in the following chapter.

## KEEPING TRACK OF PROPOSITIONS

A proposition announces something about the world. It does this by linking particular objects and concepts (italicised below) together.

Consider the following quotations from academic texts:

1. 'One attains *self-consciousness* only as he takes, or finds himself stimulated to take, *the attitude of the other.* Then he is in a position of reacting in himself to that attitude of the other.' (Mead, 1934: 194)
2. '*Power* is not an *institution*, and not a *structure*; neither is it a certain strength we are endowed with, it is the name one attributes to a *complex strategical relationship* in a particular *society*.' (Foucault, 1981: 93)
3. 'For studies of *inequalities in health* to contribute to our understanding of etiology, we need a tight focus on the pathways that lead from social and economic disadvantage to poor health, particularly if we are to meet the requirement that *social causes* of inequalities in health must be biologically plausible.' (Nazroo, 2003: 277 and 283)

Each of these quotations involves a number of propositions. The second quotation, for instance, is from Michel Foucault and deals with his general programme of research into power and social order. This quotation can be separated out into individual propositions about power:

1. Power is not an institution;
2. Power is not a structure;
3. Power is not an endowed strength;
4. Power refers to a complex strategical relationship in a particular society.

The list of short statements about power shows how each proposition makes an announcement about power.

Breaking the text down into separate propositions is a very good way to begin to engage critically with an academic article. Obviously, we cannot do this to every single paragraph in an article or a book. It would be exhausting. However, most academic texts contain important paragraphs that often function as summaries of their major propositions, as with the quotation from Foucault above. So, as you continue reading something, you can make special notes when you come to big propositions; this, in turn, will stand you in good stead when you reach a dense summarising paragraph, for your notes will help you to sort its components into separate, more easily under-stood propositions.

Propositions in sociology often connect objects and concepts together in some kind of relationship. Building on these relationships, multiple propositions are connected together into a broader argument. In order to write a good sociological essay you will need to identify the objects, concepts and propositions which have been used in the aca-demic works you have read. By doing so you should build your own argument, responding to the way in which academic authors connect objects and concepts together in their propositions and how they con-nect their propositions into a broader argument. The chances are you have already used propositions in your own essays, but might not have recognised them as such. Knowing how to identify them in the texts you read will help you work out how to use them consciously and thus effec-tively in your own writing.

Look again at the following quotation from Mead's work:

> One attains *self-consciousness* only as he takes, or finds himself stimu-lated to take, *the attitude of the other*. Then he is in a position of reacting in himself to that attitude of the other. (Mead, 1934: 194)

You can see how he links together the two main concepts in such a way that one becomes dependent on the other. He declares that 'self-consciousness' (concept 1) is only possible by taking 'the attitude of the other' (concept 2), putting oneself in their position. A critical reading of Mead shows the way to start articulating how particular concepts have been defined and then linked together in his account of social interaction and the self. He links these concepts together through making propositions about the objects with which he is con-cerned; in this example he is writing about the self. This kind of analysis provides a basis of good notes that can be used to keep track of the way Mead makes his argument and which will allow you to cre-ate concise and instructive paragraphs. For example, you could now write that:

> Mead makes an argument about how self-consciousness arises. In his account, the concept of 'the attitude of the other' is central. Mead proposes that self-consciousness is only possible when one begins to adopt the viewpoint of the other, i.e. see oneself in the way others do. This proves crucial to his account of the self.

## IDENTIFYING OBJECTS, CONCEPTS
## AND PROPOSITIONS

The extract below occurs early in Anthony Giddens' book *The Constitution of Society* and includes a number of propositions about the relationship between individual reflexivity and social organisation. These propositions are essential to a number of claims he makes later in the book. Marking out the propositions would be a useful way of setting out some of the territory of Giddens' argument. Indeed, here is a good example of how dense paragraphs full of propositions can be usefully broken down into their constituent elements in order to find ways of critically grasping what is involved.

Simply go through the paragraph and turn it into a series of propositions. It may mean modifying the sentences slightly by paraphrasing or reordering the words. This is fine so long as you keep good notes of what the original text says as well (including careful note of the page number), and as long as you write so that it is clear where you are quoting and where you are paraphrasing.

> To be a human being is to be a purposive agent, who both has reasons for his or her activities and is able, if asked, to elaborate discursively upon those reasons (including lying about them). But terms such as 'purpose' or 'intention', 'reason', 'motive' and so on have to be treated with caution, since their usage in the philosophical literature has very often been associated with a hermeneutical voluntarism, and because they extricate human action from the contextuality of time-space. Human action occurs as a *durée*, a continuous flow of conduct, as does cognition. Purposive action is not composed of an aggregate or series of separate intentions, reasons and motives. (Giddens, 1984: 3)

Breaking these kinds of dense paragraphs apart makes it possible to see how the propositions might be tackled individually. One of the first propositions in the quotation from Giddens is that 'To be a human being is to be a purposive agent who ... has reasons for his or her activities.' We might then take this individual proposition and see if there are any other theories or formulations that might offer alternative accounts. The proposition makes a connection between 'being human', 'purposive action' and 'having reasons'. In this case, the object he is concerned to define is 'human being'. Giddens uses the concept of purposeful action to make a proposition about what a human being is. A good place to develop a critical commentary of his broader conception of human life and social order, then, is to find a way to challenge or refine these particular connections, identifying whether there might be alternative definitions of his object (human being) and whether the application of his concepts (purposive action and so forth) is sensible and useful. Key to being able critically to engage with this proposition is thus to break it down further into the concepts that it links together.

It is this kind of work that you should be doing when making notes on your readings. You should keep notes on how different texts define concepts, how they are linked together in propositions and how propositions are connected into the broader argument. By doing so you will be able to find the connections that are being made in the line of argument that the authors are developing. Then you will be able to choose some of those definitions and connections to affirm, challenge or refine when creating your own argument. In essence, the development of your own argument emerges out of this process of identifying and interrogating the definitions and connections between concepts made in the existing academic literature.

## KEEPING NOTES ON CONCEPTS AND PROPOSITIONS

When reading material for an essay it is vital that you can keep clear notes on propositions and concepts. It can be useful to copy quotations from a range of sources in a consistent format to make it easier to compare across different texts and thus to build up a critical reading of those materials. You should find a structure that works best for you, although the system detailed below makes for a good start.

### The three-column system

This is a system in which you create a separate document or page for each text you include. Create a document on your computer or divide up a piece of paper into the format shown in Table 1.

#### Structure of the three-column system
**Top row:** In the top line that runs all the way across, keep a detailed note of the source. It is best to keep your notes under the heading of the reference in full, just in case your actual text goes missing or in case you get confused

**Table 1** Structure of the three-column system

| Citation in full of the source text | | |
| --- | --- | --- |
| *Direct quotations* | *Propositions and concepts* | *Ideas and references* |
| Here you will put direct quotations from the text, including page numbers. | Here you can make a summary of the propositions made in the direct quotations and note down the main concepts being used. | Here you can keep track of your own thoughts and questions, and make references back to other texts you have read. |

about which source you were reading. Keeping the full source listed at the top means that you can always be sure that you are quoting from the correct source in your essays. In any case, it is also a very good idea to write down the source as you are required to list it in the bibliography of your essays. For the majority of students of sociological studies in the UK this will be in the Harvard referencing style. It might take up some time during your reading but it will save you a lot of time later when it really matters.

**Second row:** Label the three columns in the second line of the table.

Column 1: 'Direct quotations'
Column 2: 'Propositions and concepts'
Column 3: 'Ideas and references'

## Outline of the three-column system
Column one can be used to begin to filter your readings of texts and record the more significant quotations that you wish to make use of in developing a critical account. You don't have to record everything that you read and analyse every sentence. This would take up far too much time. Instead, look for the key quotations. The important quotations you may want to keep track of could include:

- summarising paragraphs that encapsulate the main argument being made;
- propositions that define concepts;

- propositions that relate concepts to each other;
- important bits of data, both qualitative and quantitative;
- statements about how the argument relates to other scholarship.

By keeping track of these important quotations, this first column can be the primary stage of identifying the most useful material. It is essential that you keep track of which text you are quoting and which page(s) the quotation comes from, so remember to use the first line to write out the source in full, and in this first column always note the page number. This will help you to refer back to the text quickly and easily when you need to.

Column two can be used to begin to filter and break down the information you've collected in the first column. You do not have to break down all of the quotation but you should look for the key propositions being made and the key concepts involved in these propositions. This is the second stage of filtering your notes as you highlight the concepts and propositions that are most important in the quotations you select. You can choose whether to copy out quotations in column one for the whole text and then move on to columns two and three in sequence, or you can complete columns one, two and three for each quotation you take down as you read through the text. Do whichever method works best for you.

Column three can be used to keep track of your ideas as you go through your readings. As you move through your note taking you may want to return to earlier quotations you've recorded and add some ideas that have come to you as you carried on working. It can also be helpful to use the 'ideas and references' column to refer to other quotations and texts. You may want to refer back to earlier quotations you've recorded and note down your ideas of how these quotations could be linked together. Or you might want to go back to earlier quotations and refer forward to a later quotation. Finally, you may wish to refer to other sources completely, so remember to make a note of the author's name and the year of the publication as well as any relevant page numbers. This can be a good way to keep track of how different authors might support or contradict each other's propositions, and to start exploring the way in which you might begin to build an argument. This work of taking notes on propositions, concepts and your own ideas and referencing backwards and forwards will help you to make sense of the way the ideas and texts you're exploring are linked together and begin to suggest possible lines of argument to develop in your essays.

Remember to leave some room after each quotation across the table so that if you want to add more to column two or three you have space to do so afterwards.

Table 2 is an example of the three-column system used to keep track of a couple of quotations from Foucault's *History of Sexuality Volume 1*.

**Table 2** Example of the three-column system

**Source: Foucault, M. (1981) *History of Sexuality Volume 1*. New York: Pantheon Books.**

| *Quotations* | *Propositions and concepts* | *Notes and ideas* |
|---|---|---|
| Page 86<br>'Power is tolerable only on condition that it mask a substantial part of itself. Its success is proportional to its ability to hide its own mechanisms.' | • Power is tolerable only when it masks a substantial part of itself.<br>• Power's success is proportional to how well it hides its mechanisms. | • So perhaps coordinated social resistance becomes harder when power is more hidden? (see quotation from page 31)<br>• Are there examples of when power has been revealed and becomes intolerable? |
| Page 95<br>'Where there is power there is resistance and yet, or rather consequently, this resistance is never in a position of exteriority in relation to power.' | • Where there is power there is resistance.<br>• Resistance is interior to power. | • So there is no 'escape' from power even when one is resisting? Does Foucault define the concept of power too broadly?<br>• Means resistance has to be 'interior' to power too.<br>• Could challenge this proposition using Harstock's (1989: 23) critique: are we doomed to just accept domination? |

## CHAPTER SUMMARY: READING CRITICALLY AND MAKING NOTES

- In order to succeed in your essays, you need to develop a critical reading of literature. This requires reading in depth and breadth, to understand both the scope of the literature and the finer details of the issues that form the focus of your essay.
- Reading widely and in depth will help you to summarise key texts. You should be able to indicate the main argument(s) made in the text, what level of social organisation it focuses on (e.g. micro structures or macro structures), what methods and evidence it uses, and whether it is largely empirically based or theoretical.
- Reading widely and in depth will help you to locate key texts within the broader academic context. You should be able to identify the field(s) of research to which a text belongs, how it relates to other work conducted in the past or around the same time, and what the text contributed to the field and perhaps to the broader sociological literature.
- When reading you should be 'actively' engaging with the way the author makes their argument. This means looking for the evidence which they use to defend their argument and not taking what the author says at face value.
- A critical reading also means looking for the objects, concepts and propositions which make up the argument.
- Objects are the things that sociologists study, from physical things like buildings, institutions like 'the education system' or ideas like 'charity' or 'intelligence'. How a sociological object is defined might vary quite significantly across fields of research. Identifying how an academic text defines its objects is important to a critical reading of it.
- Concepts are things which sociologists use to describe and analyse sociological objects, and these too might be used differently in different areas of sociological research. Identifying the concepts which are being used in a text and how they are being defined helps you to compare and contrast academic contributions and their findings, approaches and theories.

- Propositions make statements about the world, and often link concepts and objects together. How concepts are linked together and used to examine sociological objects is part of the way academic arguments are pieced together in sociology. Identifying the most important propositions made in an argument gives you different ways in which you might use, refine or challenge an argument.
- The three-column system is a very helpful way of collecting notes on readings in a critical fashion.

# ❧ 2 ❧

# MAKING AN ARGUMENT

Writing an essay almost always involves making an argument. An argument can be understood to be a critical line of thought that runs through your essay from start to finish. It should build upon your critical reading of a set of materials and should reflect your overall position on the question posed. An argument is not just a statement of being 'for or against' something. It is true that you may sometimes wish to make an argument that takes a hard line in support of, or in opposition to, a particular theory, journal article, interpretation of some data or a political standpoint and so forth. But arguments can also be subtler, weaving together different items from your critical review of the literature, taking a more equivocal position, weighing up merits and faults and coming to a nuanced conclusion. A good argument should always take into account different ways of thinking about the issues at hand in order to arrive at an evaluation of the subject matter. It is vital that your argument should be coherent so that it holds together throughout. The argument needs to be set up at the beginning, explained and exemplified in the middle and reach a natural conclusion at the end of your essay. Remember that this is one of the key features your tutors look for in assessing your work.

All this might sound a little abstract. But arguments are not mysterious and it is likely that you already make arguments in the essays that you write without fully registering the fact. An argument is made via the overall structure of your essay and then developed in the finer detail of individual sections, paragraphs and sentences. The particular way in which you piece together and create a sequence of those theories, sources, critical viewpoints, primary data, your own thinking and whatever else appears in your essay is what is meant by your lecturers when they instruct you to make your own argument.

In the chapters that follow we examine these issues in more detail as we explore what an argument looks like in relation to the beginning, middle and end of an essay. But before going into these details it is important to examine how you can get from a critical reading of literature, together with the notes that you have made as you worked, to the basic structure of an argument. In order to do so we consider the shape of arguments in broad terms, and examine some of the typical structures that you will be required to use in writing essays. We then move to look in finer detail at the ways you can make good use of the concepts and propositions that you have identified in the literature.

## CHOOSING A STRUCTURE

Typically, your essays will involve answering a set question. Some questions will impose a structure on your argument whereas others will not – it depends on how open or specific the question is. For example, you could be asked to: 'Compare and contrast Goffman and Mead's theories of the self.' This implies quite a distinct structure, which can be called a 'compare and contrast' structure. Other questions are less specific. For example, you could be asked to: 'Explain and discuss Mead's contention that the self is fundamentally social.' This question implies some structure (you will probably be wise to explain the contention and then to discuss it), but it is less limiting and allows you to develop your own approach to the question, particularly with regard to the element of discussion. How you discuss Mead's contention is up to you but remember that the way you choose to do so will be an important part of the assessment by your tutor.

It is important to think about how the question you must answer should shape the structure of the argument that you make. If the question is closed and imposes a particular structure then that is the one to pursue. If the question is more open then it is wise to consider what kind of structure will complement the argument you wish to make that also fits well with the question.

In order to make such decisions it is helpful to be familiar with structures which are commonly used. We present a list of some of them, but it is not exhaustive. There are other forms that your argument might take. Our aim in working through these examples is to point out some of the choices and considerations you should be making when you are putting together a response to an essay question that makes a strong, clear argument. The crucial point to remember is to make sure you put some thought into deciding on an overarching structure for your essay, and that, with it, you consider how best to organise the critical reading you have done into a coherent argument as the backbone of this structure, in order to respond to the question in the best and most appropriate way. When beginning to write essays at university or college, some people find themselves writing the essay off the top of their head, with barely any forethought and not much of a plan as to how the overall argument will be organised. Stopping to think about this before you write can be a great help in ensuring that your argument is clearly laid out for the reader, and, indeed, in making sure that you actually have an argument that is substantiated. It also helps guard against including masses of material just because you have read it, but which turns out to be irrelevant simply because you have not stopped to consider whether or quite how it helps answer the question. Thinking about the structure of your argument is, then, part of how you should plan your efforts as well as being a way of getting from critical reading to a first draft. Below we present four common structures that will help you to think about good ways to shape an argument:

1. Compare and contrast
2. Build and refine
3. The author and their critics
4. Data analysis and interpretation.

## 1. 'Compare and contrast' structures

This structure generally inspects two or more items, for example theories, arguments, journal articles or sets of data. A question of this type will normally ask you to compare (how are they similar?) and contrast (how are they different?) these two items. For example, you might be asked to: 'Compare and contrast McLuhan's and Adorno's theories as applied to television.'

The compare and contrast structure is intended to shine a light on the items involved in such a way that the features of each become clearer through this comparison. Generally, a compare and contrast should not be about fine details: minor similarities or differences can usually be set aside when writing essays. Rather your essay should seek out the main similarities and differences. A good answer using this structure will also be concerned with what makes the items under consideration similar and different, for example, if they entail similar or different arguments or whether they lead to similar or different conclusions. You might want to argue that the differences, for example, are a result of the kinds of data that they use, the kind of methodological approach they take, the kinds of political project involved, the audience they were written for or indeed the period when they were written and more. In this way you piece together the similarities and differences, linking them into a broader argument.

The key dimension to this structure is that you make sure that you compare *and* contrast. Some student essays that ought to adopt a compare and contrast structure depend far too heavily on only one of them, or neglect one of them by leaving it to the conclusion. A compare and contrast structure does not have to be split equally into two, half comparison and half contrast, but they should be reasonably weighted to ensure that you make a decent consideration on each side. Both are needed.

This relates to the second consideration you should make when deciding whether to collect all of the comparisons together into one section of your essay and all of the contrasts into another, or whether to instead compare and contrast the items point by point. As a rough guide, students usually collect all the similarities together followed by all the differences if the two items to be compared and contrasted are, broadly, quite similar. This allows you to show that the items under consideration (the theories, periods, sets of data, etc.) are broadly more similar than they are different, and to make a conclusion which states this argument. When the comparison is less stark, it is generally easier to take issues in your comparison one at a time, exploring how the items are similar or different to each other point by point, thereby supporting a more nuanced conclusion.

You might be given the two items to compare and contrast, or you might be asked to make your own selections, for example from a list of papers, topics or theorists. The key question to bear in mind when making your own selection is how much or how little do these items have in common? If you choose two that are very similar then there will not be much to learn from this. It might be better to find items that are a little more different and so can be more effectively compared and contrasted. If they are too different from each other, then you risk struggling to make a good argument simply because the differences may be too many or too obvious.

The best way of putting together your argument in a 'compare and contrast' structure is to use the concepts and propositions you have uncovered in your critical reading of the literature, a tactic which also applies to the other structures we review in this chapter. You can best make use of concepts and propositions in this kind of structure simply by organising some of your comparisons and contrasts directly in relation to the very concepts and propositions you have identified. To return to our example of the comparison between McLuhan's and Adorno's theories of television, you might find that they use different concepts (e.g. the 'cool media' and 'culture industry', respectively). Your analysis could then outline the kinds of propositions they develop by applying these concepts to the object of analysis (television). Outlining how they apply their concepts to the object of analysis can lead you to evaluate their analyses in light of what they conclude about television, for example, does it increase creative participation from viewers or immobilise them? Thinking in terms of how the articles have used concepts and propositions in this way allows you to draw more sophisticated contrasts and comparisons by helping you to identify why these items are similar and different. So, this is the kind of work that represents how you make your argument.

In a compare and contrast structure it can help both you and your reader to indicate in your beginning paragraph(s) what items you intend to compare and contrast, especially if this has not been made explicit in the question. Adding the reason for your selection is even better. For example, perhaps you intend to compare and contrast X with Y because they provide an effective comparison to help you to exemplify some of the important features of the topic at hand. But whatever the reason, it is important to take care that it links to both the essay question and to the argument that you go on to make. Then you should very briefly describe in what ways your chosen items are similar or different and how your argument will be developed by virtue of making this comparison (see Chapter 3 on beginnings for more information on how to write a guide to your argument in your opening paragraphs).

A 'compare and contrast' structure such as this may lead you to a conclusion that stands in favour of one of the items on some particular issue. If it does, then always be very sure to give reasons for your judgement, even if briefly. So, for instance, you might conclude that one theory is better than another, or one journal article is better than another. It is also possible to conclude that both items contribute to understanding an issue but that they do so in different, possibly complementary ways. Whatever the result, it is important that the conclusion clearly develops from the comparisons and contrasts that you have made. Remember you should try very hard to go beyond merely concluding that there are similarities and differences. Try to explore why there are similarities and differences, or what effects such similarities or differences might have, for example on our academic understanding of the subject, or what implications it all might have for some practical, political or ethical issue, or for future work in the area.

## 2. 'Build and refine' structures

When you are not asked to compare and contrast material you may commonly find that you are being asked to build an argument by piecing together material you have studied in the course and encountered in your additional readings, and to reflect on this material in some way. In order to construct this type of essay you will need to draw on a number of items from your critical review of the literature, selecting those that can fit well together and contribute to your argument. In this case the emphasis will be on how each journal article, book or chapter that you consider adds something extra to your analysis. In this regard you build and refine your argument paragraph by paragraph, taking the reader through the series of readings and/or selections of data you have chosen to present, signposting the direction of your argument as you go. For example, a build and refine structure would be appropriate in response to the question: 'Describe how black feminism has contributed to the development of feminism more broadly.' Here you might present the work of several authors who have contributed to black feminism, perhaps by building up chronologically or maybe thematically, drawing in quotations from the literature together with your interpretations of it, all the time instructing the reader along the way as to how these selections develop and evidence your broader argument. A 'compare and contrast' structure would be inappropriate for this type of question, because instead of asking you to focus on two or three items it requires you to explore the literature more broadly.

Common elements to include in a 'build and refine' structure are theories, data and examples. One possible build and refine structure would be to introduce a theory, then add to this by referring to some data, going on to refine it further with reference to a second theory, finishing off with an example of the way the two theories between them make better sense of the data than either on its own. Of course, it need not follow this pattern, and it is up to you to determine which elements to use to build and refine your argument, and in which order they should appear. But such a structure is typically created by including materials from several different academic sources rather than focusing upon only one or two authors.

The key task when constructing such an essay is to organise the sequence of elements that you will present, those being the quotations from the literature, analogies you wish to make, selections of data and so forth. You must sequence these elements so that each one builds on the previous one, developing your argument further at each stage on the way to the conclusion. Sometimes you will want to include material from your critical reading that you happen to like very much or that you think is particularly interesting, but it does not fit, or it repeats a point that you have already made. In this situation it can be just as important to decide to leave out material as it can be to decide to include it. Make sure that you only include elements in your structure because they build on the argument by adding something new and important, or by refining something that has already been considered. If you find that you would like to add some material but it merely repeats an earlier point, then you need to think about which source helps you to make the point more clearly and more effectively for your current essay and incorporate that one. You can always very briefly refer to the other to note that it runs along similar lines. Alternatively, a more detailed solution might be to merge the presentation of the two materials, but take care only to do so if it clearly helps to bolster the argument. Certainly it is common to mix sources in a paragraph in different ways. For example, if three academic articles make a similar argument then it might well be enough to put the argument into your own words, cite all the articles, but draw primarily on one source by, for example, including a direct quotation.

You can use concepts and propositions most effectively in this kind of structure by ensuring that a number of the elements that you incorporate into your argument contribute to its development by introducing, defining, exemplifying, refining, challenging or countering a concept or proposition made in the literature concerning your objects of interest. For example, your answer to the question on black feminism might begin with a central proposition such as 'feminism has ignored differences between women's experiences of patriarchy'. You could then build upon this by introducing new concepts developed by black feminists that help to address this proposition, such as bringing the concept of racial discrimination into feminism. Thereafter you could further refine this argument, for example, by introducing the concept of intersectionality as a way of moving towards an understanding of how gender and ethnicity are entangled.

In writing your essay's beginning paragraphs in a 'build and refine' structure it is often a good idea to mention some of the key elements you will be using to construct your argument. Thereafter you should briefly outline what each element adds and mention how this allows you to build an argument leading to a particular conclusion (again, see Chapter 3 on beginnings for more information on how to write a guide to your argument in your opening paragraphs).

## 3. The author and their critics

Sociology tutors frequently set essay questions which ask you to describe and assess one theory or another. For example, you could be asked to: 'Evaluate Weeks et al.'s theory of families of choice.' The common way to critically evaluate a theory is to explore how other academics have received it, taking account of both positive and negative reactions, and how it has been used, modified or rejected. In doing so you can summarise some of its strengths and weaknesses. Remember that a critical analysis is not negative, but rather it is evaluative, even if your evaluation turns out to be negative. What is important is to weigh up strengths as well as weaknesses in light of a careful consideration of all the concepts and propositions put forward.

In this respect, you can best critically evaluate a theory by attending to how an author has developed and linked the concepts and associated propositions they present (as described in Chapter 1 on reading critically). You should ask yourself how the author arrived at their position and what evidence they have drawn on to do so. Consider how and why certain elements of the theory have been adopted, modified, challenged or rejected since its original statement and initial reception in the literature. You can then evaluate concepts and propositions in the theory by examining how subsequent work has sought to use or to redefine the concepts, and the way other academics have upheld or challenged the connections made between concepts in the theorist's key propositions. You might also examine how other academics have affirmed or contested the propositions made in the theory, whether on the basis of more abstract discussion or their own investigations and empirical evidence.

When reading the material to prepare a structure such as this, it is handy to have the following questions in mind:

- How coherent is the theory? Do the concepts link together in useful ways?
- How well substantiated is the theory? Is there a good fit between the argument and the evidence?
- How important is the theory? Does it help to analyse a range of different patterns or practices of the social world or is it quite narrow in scope?
- How 'complementary' is the theory? Can it be used alongside other theories or is it only useful in isolation, and therefore is it difficult to see how it can be used within the broader set of research findings and perspectives in the literature?

Using your materials to ask questions such as these should allow you to weigh up the value of the theory in light of its concepts and propositions as well as its broader argument and so to construct your own critical evaluation. How you organise your argument as a response to any arguments presented by an academic author and their critics is by virtue of this work. Your job is to interrogate the theory, explore how others have done so and come to a view on the theory based closely on these evaluations. Your argument needs to be clearly shaped by the critical investigation you have conducted; your view is not simply an opinion you happen to have, but must be carefully tied in to your reading.

When bringing together a critical evaluation of a theory in this way it is important to ensure that you proceed through the essay in a sensible and organised fashion. In this kind of structure more than any other, the decisions about the order in which you present the various elements of your argument are yours to make. So it is not surprising that students most commonly get lost in this kind of essay, leaving the reader confusedly trying to work their way through a badly structured piece of writing with a weak conclusion. Too many students jump wildly from one issue to another because they have failed to think carefully about the order in which they should make their case. Often this is made worse by not having devoted enough time to constructing their own argument through a critical reading of the author's academic texts. Thus you must take great care – and make the time – to ensure that you create your own argument and that you present it in an appropriately ordered fashion.

There are at least two major structures you can choose between when evaluating a theory. In both structures it is usual to begin by outlining the main points of the theory and by situating it within an academic context and/or within the body of work of the author. Then, however, you have to make a choice. You can decide to deal with all the strengths of the theory together, followed by all the weaknesses grouped together. This structure might be particularly suited to an essay in which you wish to present an argument about how divided the academic community is on an issue. For instance, you might find that there are two 'camps' – one of detractors, the other of advocates of the theory. Presenting one and then the other means you can evaluate the theory quite well, at the same time as also exemplifying the divided way the theory has been received. You should take care, however, that you are not portraying academics as advocates or detractors simply for the sake of your essay. Some academic theories do, of course, prompt polarised reactions and you may find that there are indeed clearly divided camps. But do remember that it is just as common to find that academics have responded to a theory in a more even-handed fashion, weighing up the positives and negatives in much the way that you must. Where this is the case you can choose to proceed by going into more detail on specific elements of the theory, providing a critical review of each issue you present by weighing up the strengths and weaknesses, and reporting how they have each been received by other academics. This might be particularly suited to an essay in which you wish to tackle a few separate parts of a theory, one at a time, evaluating as you go along. Creating this sort of structure can save you repeating yourself by having to revisit the same issue, as you would need to do if you decided to present all the strengths together, followed by all the weaknesses.

In writing the beginning paragraphs for an 'author and their critics' type of structure, it could be a good idea to indicate which are the main issues, as well as the key concepts and propositions that you will be exploring, and which critics' work you will be using to evaluate these concepts and propositions. You should also indicate what your conclusion will be. With either structure you can conclude by arguing, on balance, how successful you think the theory is in terms of the series of questions provided earlier, along with a brief report on how well the theory has been received in the academic literature. You can also state whether you think the reception is justified, or note that you disagree and explain why (as before, look at Chapter 3 on beginnings for suggestions on how to write a guide to your argument in your opening paragraphs).

## 4. Data interpretation and analysis

Some essay questions will ask you to interrogate data, or to evaluate claims that are based on data, no matter what form the data take. You could be asked, for example, to: 'Select three questions from the 2015 British Social Attitudes Survey, describe the results and interpret the findings in light of relevant academic research.' While this book is not about analysing data, there are some common features to data interpretation and analysis that are worth discussing here since they cohere around a fairly standard way of organising an essay. A 'data interpretation and analysis' structure should generally involve several elements, moving, in most cases, through the following:

1. Some description of the study design, how the data were collected, what kind of data you are dealing with and what their limitations are;
2. Presentation of the data most relevant to the essay question, for example, quotations, selections from ethnographic field notes, graphs, charts, tables;
3. Some interpretation of these representations that explains to the reader what it is that the data show, for example, what does the quotation tell you about a particular subject, or what pattern does a graph show?
4. Some subsequent analysis of this information which places it into context and explains what the interpretation of the data helps us to understand about the issue under consideration.

These elements do not always correspond to four distinct sections, proceeding one after the other. Instead, you might find yourself needing to move back and forth between the last three depending upon the scope of the data and the question you have been asked. Returning to our example about analysing three questions from the British Social Attitudes Survey, for instance, you might proceed from 1 to 4 for all three of the questions together, or you might start with step 1 for all three, then move through steps 2–4 for each question individually. This is a decision you need to make in light of the particular essay question.

The important factor to consider in deciding which order to use will be to determine which is the best way of conveying to your reader the clearest possible idea of the direction in which your inquiries into the data have led. Depending on the question, you may be required to situate the data in the academic literature. Questions that ask you to analyse and evaluate data are likely to require you to use existing work to interpret and critically engage with the data, and to report how well the data can be used to evaluate the concepts and propositions in the literature. This is where you can best make use of concepts and propositions from your critical reading of relevant literature by linking them directly to the data. You might consider, for instance, how the data depend upon a particular definition of a concept (e.g. ethnicity or class) and explore the implications of defining the concept differently. Or you might examine how the data can help you to evaluate concepts and propositions already in the literature. For example, you might show that the data you have analysed undermine or substantiate particular propositions made in the literature on crime or ethnicity, gender or class and so forth. This could lead you to conclude that the data support one academic perspective over another, or both equally, or neither (again, see Chapter 3 on beginnings for additional discussion of the way to write a guide to your argument in your opening paragraphs).

## DETAILED ARGUMENT TECHNIQUES

In this section we consider how to construct the finer detail of your argument using some techniques that will make the best use of your critical reading. These techniques are based on the way you can use concepts and propositions, link them together, reflect on them and consider their relation to one another in order to describe and examine social phenomena and thus to develop a critical argument throughout your work.

### Defining and exemplifying objects and concepts

You will find that almost every essay you write involves the definition of some objects and key concepts. Whether you are writing a purely theoretical essay or one based on empirical material, you will need to describe to the reader which objects you will be writing about and to explain the meanings of the key concepts that you use to examine these phenomena.

For example, you might be writing an essay that examines the impacts that social media have had on everyday life. Social media are the objects that you will be writing about. There is a range of different concepts that you might use to explore the object of social media, for example Castells' (2009) concept of 'network society'. It is helpful to be able to explain to the reader that you will focus on a particular object, which might be stipulated in the essay question or might be of your choice. Defining and exemplifying your objects is crucial to helping set the boundaries for your essay and to inform your reader as to how your answer will tackle the question.

One way to ensure that you define your objects adequately is to draw on your critical reading of the academic literature. The following example from a student's essay shows how he explains that the objects he will be writing about are 'social movement organisations' and uses a quotation from the literature to define these kinds of objects. And to explain the objects you are writing about still further, it can be helpful to provide an example of them. In the extract below, the student has also done well to exemplify the object of social movement organisations:

> This essay will focus on social movement organisations, which are 'a complex, or formal, organisation which identifies its goals with the preferences of a social movement or a countermovement and attempts to implement those goals.' (McCarthy and Zald, 1977: 1218) I will be focussing in this essay on the social movement organisation 'Invisible Children', which was behind the campaign to arrest Joseph Kony. [Quotation from a third-year sociology student's essay]

You can see in this example that the student has quoted McCarthy and Zald's paper in order to show the source of his description of social movement organisations and to tie the definition of this object into the academic literature.

Since social objects can be understood differently in different contexts and across different time frames, it is often useful to instruct readers in how you will be defining your object of interest in relation to other possible definitions. Here is an example from a student's essay on whether friendships have become interchangeable with kin relationships in Western societies, in which the student discusses some different interpretations of 'friend':

> First, in understanding how friends can be seen to be interchangeable with kin as valued personal relationships, the term's meaning must first

be defined. 'Friend' is a cultural phenomenon that changes over time and space. In Western society, it is customary to understand friendship as simply a human personal attachment (O'Connor, 1992, p. 7) that offers something more intimate than acquaintanceship. Davies (2011) discusses how images of friendship like this within Western culture are perpetuated as being highly positive. 'Friend' tends to be described as a supportive, mutually beneficial and reciprocal relationship (Smart et al, 2012). Popular culture heightens these images through television programmes such as 'Friends' and 'Sex and the City', showing homogenous friendship groups acting as support-systems for one another in a family-like setting (Davies, 2011). In this essay I will argue that friendships have become more like kin relationships but that they do not represent the idealised image presented. [Quotation from a third-year sociology student's essay]

Here the student has linked the definition of the object to the question that she is going to answer, explored the definition of friendship using several sources and highlighted certain features of friendship using examples from popular culture.

You should also define and explain the concepts that you will use to explore your objects of interest. This is particularly important when the concept you are defining is central to your argument and to the way you approach the question. Defining a concept should also usually be supported by a reference to the academic literature. In the previous chapter we explored how you can keep track of concepts and propositions as you engage in a critical reading of the academic literature. We discussed how concepts can be defined in more than one way, or even several quite different ways, depending upon the manner in which academics use them. Consider, for example, how social theorists have used the terms 'power', 'self' or 'agency' differently. Rather than fretting about which is 'right' or 'best', you are more likely to use such differences as an important part of your argument, in, for example, a 'compare and contrast' or an 'author and their critics' structure. It is important to tie your definition of concepts to a particular academic journal article or book in order to engage in this kind of evaluative work. You will find that it is sometimes helpful to use a quotation from an academic source to help you to explain the concept. This is because it shows the person marking your work that you have done some reading to try to understand the concept, and also that you intend to use the concept in a particular way.

However, you should not just rely on a quotation to do the work of defining the concept for you; you should also discuss it. Indeed, it is usually important not just to define but also to explain and exemplify concepts, particularly if they are fairly difficult to understand or if the exemplification can help to tie the concept into the argument being developed in the essay. By exemplification in this case we mean using an example to show what the concept means or further explain how the concept is used to examine social objects.

As with defining your objects of interest, you should generally relate the definition and exemplification of your concepts to the question that you are answering and so also to your argument. In the example below you can see how a student has outlined a concept from Bauman's (2015) research and connected it to the question by showing how she will apply the concept to the essay's object of interest, namely, immigration. In the first paragraph of the essay, the student introduced the concept of 'new racism'; in this second paragraph she introduces the concept of 'liquid modernity' and ties it into her developing argument.

> Against a fragmented realm of competing identities, Bauman's concept of 'liquid modernity' implies a rootlessness for contemporary subjects. Uncertainties that walk hand-in-hand with globalisation have enabled subjects to shift easily from one social position to another in a flexible manner, meaning individually-chosen identities replace traditional patterns (Bauman, 2015). I endeavour to build on these ideas and assess whether political attitudes towards immigration are premised on notions of a 'new racism' based on cultural differences, and whether previously fixed national identities have been eroded over time. [Quotation from a third-year sociology student's essay]

This example demonstrates the importance of defining concepts and relating them to the question that you are answering by applying them to your objects of interest. It also begins to illustrate the power of connecting concepts together.

## Connecting concepts

In order to begin building your argument it is often necessary to connect concepts from your critical reading of the relevant literature. When linking concepts you are generally aiming to paint a picture of the argument that is being made in the literature. How you do this forms part of your own argument since you will have to make decisions about which concepts are most important to include, how to connect them, which ones to highlight and which to leave in the background, and which contributions to the literature you want to use for the purpose. This exemplifies some of the decision-making and critical thinking that your tutor, or whoever is marking your essay, is looking for when they assess your work. In the extract below you should be able to identify how the student has linked three readings together by outlining the way each has a bearing on the study of women's labour.

> With increasing amounts of women entering paid work Walby (1996) argued that women were now doing a 'dual shift' by both caring for the house and being involved in gainful employment. Walby argues that women end up working more hours in the day, with little further domestic work being conducted by men to aid them. Even when men were unemployed and women worked, Grint (2005: 231) notes that 'there is little evidence of unemployed men using their "free" time to take over domestic responsibilities from their "working" wives.' Furthering Walby's point, Duncombe and Marsden (1995) argue that women actually perform a 'triple shift', made up of paid work, emotional labour, and housework and childcare, for which they have little reward. [Quotation from a second-year sociology student's essay]

Here you can see how the student connects together complementary observations and concepts from the literature and builds up a picture of the way in which academics have studied and conceptualised labour demands on women. The student outlines Walby's idea of the 'dual shift', refines this using Grint's observations, and develops the argument further by linking Walby's argument to Duncombe and Marsden's concept of the 'triple shift'. By connecting concepts together in this way, the student begins to develop her own argument. She has clearly found several key concepts and propositions during her critical reading of the literature and has decided to connect them together into her argument – to worthwhile effect.

## Identifying connections between concepts and propositions

The previous section has shown how you can use your critical reading of the literature and note taking to identify concepts and define, exemplify and connect them. In a similar way you can then go on to identify propositions in the literature, since the manner in which academics define their concepts and link them together is an important part of how they put forward propositions and make their arguments. Identifying definitions in the academic literature usually involves detecting some important propositions as well, since those definitions typically entail claims about how things are or are not related. However, academic propositions do not always take the form of definitions. Indeed, much academic work uses concepts that have already been defined in order to develop additional propositions concerning the objects of interest. So you will often be engaged in identifying how academics connect concepts in their arguments, not just showing how they have defined them. Moreover, just as academics connect concepts together to make propositions, they also connect together propositions to make their arguments.

In the following example you can see how a student has identified a proposition put forward by Mancur Olson as part of his argument about rational action theory.

> Mancur Olson's (1965) 'rational action theory' suggested that rational individuals would not protest if the costs were high and they could reap the benefits of protests won by social movements just by being 'free riders' and taking no action themselves. As such, Olson argued that people would only take part in collective action when the costs were reduced and the benefits increased, so movements should supply secondary benefits, which he termed 'selective incentives', which would encourage action from participants. [Quotation from a third-year sociology student's essay]

Here we can see how the student identifies four propositions made by Olson:

1. Rational individuals would not protest if the costs were high.
2. They could reap the benefits of protests won by social movements just by being 'free riders' and taking no action themselves.
3. People would only take part in collective action when the costs were reduced and the benefits increased.
4. Therefore, movements should supply secondary benefits, which he termed 'selective incentives', which would encourage action from participants.

The fourth proposition also includes a definition of a concept, namely 'selective incentives'. Breaking this paragraph down into the propositions can help you to see the way you can build a paragraph from your own breakdown of academic texts into concepts and propositions (as we showed in Chapter 1 on critical reading and note taking). By illustrating the way Olson connected these propositions in his development of the rational action theory of social movement organisations, the student is able to go on to challenge Olson's account in the rest of the essay. He does so first by identifying which of these propositions he disagrees with, and then by showing that if you do not accept certain of Olson's propositions then the others lose power because, in his account, they are all dependent upon each other.

Showing that certain concepts are linked into a coherent scheme is not the only way to identify how an academic connects concepts and propositions in their argument. In the following example from a student's essay on Foucault's theories of power, you can see how she identifies two different concepts of power in Foucault's work, showing the different propositions he makes about them, in order to evidence the way in which Foucault compares and contrasts them:

Sovereign power is the absolute power exercised by monarchs in the feudal, pre-Enlightenment world – which Foucault defines as the 'power to take life or let live' (Foucault, 1998:135). The king with his dazzling robes and jewels, would rule autocratically by legitimately waging war (1998:135). Such power acted as 'a subtraction mechanism, a right to appropriate a portion of the wealth, a tax of products, goods and services … it culminated in the privilege to seize hold of life in order to suppress it' (Foucault, 1998:136). Whether through bloody execution, or the taxation of the farmer's turnips, deduction limited unacceptable actions through the fear of punishment. Foucault argues that the technological and scientific advances of the Enlightenment, culminating in the 1789 French Revolution, opened a different world which rejected irrational traditional systems in favour of reasonable methods. This pivotal moment of optimism, spawned utopian ideas (Fourier's Phalanstery and Ledoux's ideal circular salt works) (Foucault, 1991:214) as a response to disordered and overcrowded industrial cities. Now, a new kind of power emerged: bio-power. Rather than subtracting life, bio-power *penetrates* life in a positive and productive fashion to 'incite, reinforce, control, monitor, optimize and organize the forces' (Foucault, 1998:136). So, rather than passively letting life wander or controlling it through fear of punishment, bio-power *invests* in life, establishing productive and efficient subjects in the emerging capitalist world. Bio-power seeks to ensure there is *more* life and *better* life. [Quotation from a second-year sociology student's essay]

The student does a good job of evidencing two different kinds of power in Foucault's writing, showing that he makes different propositions about how these kinds of power function, and that these two kinds of power are to be contrasted with each other in the manner in which he builds his argument. After setting out this account of Foucault's theories of power, the student goes on to argue that Foucault's research builds a convincing picture of how power has changed and with what consequences for the ways in which human beings are governed.

Explaining how academics have linked together propositions is an important part of making your own logical arguments. Grasping this allows you to go on to use propositions from the academic literature yourself, to refine them, challenge them or reject them according to whatever argument you want to build in response to the question you are tackling.

## Connecting concepts and propositions in your argument

As already pointed out, in order to use the academic literature effectively, you must be able to identify how academics use concepts to make propositions about their objects of interest, and how they link propositions together into an argument. This is why critical reading and note taking is particularly important, since you will have to be able to pick out concepts and propositions from your critical reading of the literature for exploration in your essays. How you link together concepts and propositions to represent the arguments being made by academics is also a crucial part of answering the question and developing your own argument.

In the second example below the student has been asked to: 'Use a theory from the course to interrogate the success or failure of a social movement of your choice.' The student has done an excellent job of defining and connecting concepts, of identifying propositions and of showing how Manuel Castells links these propositions together into his argument regarding the concept of 'network society':

> According to Manuel Castells we now live in what he has termed 'The Network Society.' Castells' theory of the network society can be used to explain some aspects of the Occupy movement. Castells defines the network society as a society whose social structure is made around 'networks activated by micro-electronics-based, digitally processed information and communication technologies.' (Castells, 2009: 24) A network is understood to be a web-like structure with various nodes that are connected to each other (Balleria, 2012: 4). He argues that society is moving from a hierarchical, vertical structure to a network structure. Castells also argues that the way people think determines the norms and values upon which society is constructed; power is in the minds of the people (Castells, 2007: 238). In the network society, the increasing advancement of communication technology is extending the reach of the communication media into every aspect of our lives and thus the battle for power is increasingly being fought in the domain of communication and how it shapes how people think (Castells, 2007: 239). These power relations are embedded within a global network and so resistance to them, what Castells terms 'counter-power', must also be on a global level (Castells, 2007: 249). I argue that Castells' concepts of network society and counter power help to explain why the Occupy movement was successful in some ways but not in others. [Quotation from a third-year sociology student's essay]

This example shows how careful reading and note taking can allow you to use the techniques of defining concepts, identifying propositions and connecting concepts to explain how an academic has built their argument, and to do so in such a way as to begin to put forward your own argument in response to an essay question. This is a good example to take a bit further, breaking it down into some of its constituent parts so that you can see more clearly how the techniques are being used and how they work to construct the student's argument.

The student defines the concept of the network society by using a quotation from Castells:

> Castells defines this as a society whose social structure is made around 'networks activated by micro-electronics-based, digitally processed information and communication technologies.' (Castells, 2009: 24)

She then identifies a proposition Castells makes which is based on the concept that has just been defined:

> He argues that society is moving from a hierarchical, vertical structure to a network structure.

The student goes on to identify another proposition made by Castells:

> Castells also argues that the way people think determines the norms and values upon which society is constructed; power is in the minds of the people (Castells, 2007: 238).

At this point, the student brings together these two propositions to link them to the main concept of network society (referencing the exact location in Castells's work):

> In the network society, the increasing advancement of communication technology is extending the reach of the communication media into every aspect of our lives and thus the battle for power is increasingly being fought in the domain of communication and how it shapes how people think (Castells, 2007: 239).

In yet another development the student then adds a further proposition and a concept that help extend the argument in this paragraph and starts to bring it round to link more closely to the essay question about social movements:

> These power relations are embedded within a global network and so resistance to them, what Castells terms 'counter-power' must also be on a global level (Castells, 2007: 249).

The student finishes the paragraph by making her own argument plain, explicitly linking Castells' concepts and propositions to the question she is answering in the essay:

> I argue that this helps to explain why the Occupy movement was successful in some ways but not in others.

Unpicking this example shows that it is possible to put together strong analytical paragraphs based on critical reading and note taking along with the techniques reviewed in this chapter so far. This particular student has thought very carefully about which of Castells' concepts and propositions she wants to use, and has presented them in such a way that they provide a coherent set for examining the object of interest, namely the social movement 'Occupy'.

If you use the three-column system for note taking detailed in the chapter on critical reading (Chapter 1), your notes on the way the concepts and propositions you are identifying as you read can be linked up or contrasted with one another. Thoughts on these kinds of connections could be listed in the third column, allowing you to build up elements to begin constructing your argument in the same way that the student has in the example above. And by making the notes as you are reading you are also giving yourself easy access to all the possible elements that you might use to construct the fine detail and the overall structure of your argument. Indeed, it can be invaluable to make notes about what you want to do with the sources you are reading while making your usual notes on them. Even if you end up changing your mind when returning to the notes you have made, doing so can still be very useful in sorting out your thoughts.

The student's argument about social movements emerges directly from the way she presented the concepts and propositions that Castells uses. It is clear that she has identified concepts and propositions that Castells is using from her own reading, but she has taken care not to refer to everything that Castells has to say. Indeed, the book from which the student is quoting is quite dense, with a great many concepts and plenty of different arguments. Part of the way the student has constructed her own argument is by judiciously selecting materials that can be shown to be relevant.

You will have noticed that the student has also thought about how she might want to use this selection to construct her own argument about Occupy. You can see in the extract below, which comes from the middle of the essay, how she goes on to use the concepts and propositions she has identified in Castells' work directly in relation to Occupy. This helps her build her own argument by a critical engagement with Castells whilst relating these materials directly to the question.

The success of anti-globalisation movements such as Occupy has been understood to be because of its use of networking communication technologies (Halvorsen, 2012: 430). Occupy is organised as a loosely structured, decentralised, horizontal organisation (Giugni et al., 2006: 12). This form of network organisation allows them to operate on both a small scale local level as well as on a large global scale. As Castells argued, this is important because it is necessary for counter-power to be organised at the same level as power is exercised in the network society. [Quotation from a third-year sociology student's essay]

This clearly expands upon the student's writing in the previous example, and you should be able to see that this represents a development in the essay's argument. It uses more sources from the critical literature review, which provides detail on the Occupy movement, and connects them to the student's own argument that Castells' concepts of network society and counter-power are useful in understanding Occupy. In this regard, you can see how identifying propositions in the literature and linking them to the essay question can help you to develop your own argument. In this example the student adopts Castells' proposition and applies it. However, elsewhere in the essay the student also disagrees with parts of Castells' argument about the network society. Using examples the student shows how Castells' argument does not accurately reflect the hierarchical realities of social movement organisations.

Bear in mind the important point that your own argument, which you build through the structure of your essay, does not have to mirror arguments presented in the literature. Instead, your critical appraisal of the literature can help you to use some or other concept and proposition to challenge and/or refine as part of your answer to an essay question.

## Comparing and contrasting propositions

One way in which you can effectively use concepts and propositions you have identified from the literature is by comparing and contrasting them with each other. In the example below the student has drawn a comparison and a contrast between three academic sources in order to explain the argument that she will develop in her own discussion. The question the student has been posed is: 'To what extent have same-sex relationships become organised through families of choice?'

Weeks et al. (2001) argued that same-sex relationships operate outside heterosexual norms, constructing new forms of identity and relationality for their intimate and otherwise important relationships based on 'families of choice.' Their study suggests that non-heterosexual relationships are more open, opportunistic and are constituted around individuals who are important to them, and do not follow traditional conceptions of family based on blood ties or other heterosexual relational scripts, which are often seen as constraining and structurally unequal. They situate their study in a wider literature, related to what Giddens (1992) has termed the 'pure relationship', which is more egalitarian and equal and represents 'a version of love in which a persons' sexuality is one factor that has to be negotiated as part of a relationship.' (Giddens, 1992: 63) However, more recent research by Heaphy et al. (2013: 166) has found that couples modelled their relationships 'on a concept of the ordinary rather than the radically different.' An emphasis on ordinary everyday activities in which they took part suggests there has been a change in the negotiation and practices of same sex relationships. This essay argues that there has been a shift in how same sex couples experience relationships as well as everyday activities, and that this is attributable to the changing status of same sex relationships with the introduction of Civil Partnerships in 2005 and, more recently, marriage being extended to same sex couples. [Quotation from a third-year sociology student's essay]

First, the student has outlined the propositions made by Weeks et al. in relation to the concept of 'families of choice'. Second, she has compared this with Giddens' concept of the 'pure relationship' in order to show that Weeks et al. contributed to the development of an argument about same-sex intimacies. Third, she moves on to contrast these two arguments with a third (developed by Heaphy et al.) that argues against these positions based on data that have been collected more recently. In this instance, the comparisons and contrasts work effectively to shine a light on the arguments being made about non-heterosexual relationships at the same time as showing why these arguments differ. Finally, based on these comparisons and contrasts the student is able to state clearly what the argument of her own essay is going to be. In the remainder of her essay the student moves on to explore how each of these three academic arguments can be used to understand same-sex intimacies before concluding that recent changes in governance may be behind the differences observed in the data.

This example shows how the key elements of an argument's structure can be explained to the reader in such a way as to provide an overview of the argument that you will be making in your essay, an approach to summarising an argument to be considered in the chapter on 'beginnings' (Chapter 3). For now it is most important to note that the student develops a response to the question by piecing together concepts and propositions from their reading of the literature by comparing and contrasting them. This level of work is only possible because the student has clearly thought about the literature in some detail by paying attention to the way links can be made between the arguments that they come across in their reading. This, then, is another example of how important it is to construct your own argument in relation to those arguments developed in the academic literature by identifying, explicating, connecting, comparing and contrasting concepts and propositions.

## REDRAFTING YOUR ARGUMENT

As we indicated in the Introduction to this book, it is vital that you learn to put reading and writing to multiple purposes. In writing the first draft you will likely explore the concepts and propositions you have found in the literature, you will make some of your own points and you will do a great deal of thinking. You will usually end this stage with a bit of a mixture. You might well like some parts of what you have written, but be much less happy with others; you might have written some good clear sections, but realise that others are confused and confusing; you will be satisfied with some points which are well-evidenced, whereas others are left as mere unsupported assertions. All the same, no matter what combination this mix consists of, your work in the first draft should help you to firmly determine your argument.

It is crucial that in moving from the first draft to the second draft, you actually redraft the work to make the argument clearly, rather than only making a few slight alterations. Redrafting may involve rewriting several sentences, creating different breaks between paragraphs or even reorganising whole sections. Once again, this means giving yourself enough time to reflect on what you have written and then to make decisions about what you think the argument should now be.

To make such decisions it is helpful to write out your argument in short form. As you read through the first draft, list in note form all the points that you make in the essay along with the evidence that you are using. Metaphorically, this is the map of your argument, in that it shows all the places that you have been to and the things that you have seen. Take care to keep this document short, probably no more than an A4 page. Doing so will allow you to see what you have at a quick glance and to keep a summary of it all easily in mind. You should then select those elements of your argument that are essential to hold together the main thread of your essay and keep a tight, clear shape.

You should also delete those points or perhaps even entire paragraphs or sections that are less useful or perhaps now have become irrelevant. This sort of pruning is important, sharpening your writing so that it makes a clear argument. It can, however, mean letting go of material that you like, which many of us find hard (see Chapter 13, 'How to cut your essay down to length'). Sometimes, when reading through your essay, it can be difficult to determine whether you need the material or not. This often happens if you cannot work out what you are arguing in a given sentence or paragraph. It is helpful to return to your notes or to the sources on which the material is based. Think about what you have said at an earlier stage in the essay as well as what comes immediately afterwards. Does it all follow on? If those sections before and afterwards follow from one another without the material that is giving you trouble, that material is probably unnecessary and you should just delete it. But if what comes before and after does not follow smoothly, then you should think about what needs to be said, shown or asked in order to connect them smoothly. Think about the argument of the whole section with which you are dealing. If this does not help, there is a good chance that you are still not quite sure what you are trying to argue overall. If that is the case, it means going back a stage or so and returning to the map of your argument to think again about what the essay should be arguing in response to the question.

A helpful way to test whether a particular point or paragraph is useful or not is to check what kind of contribution the text makes to the structures and techniques of argument already discussed. If the point fails to define, exemplify, use, compare, contrast or evaluate a concept or proposition, then it is likely that it is not adding enough. Think about how you can make better use of the point. For example, if the passage in question defines a concept which you then hardly mention further, then weigh up whether you need it at all. If you decide you do need it then consider exemplifying it and work out how it can be connected to other concepts or propositions which you include and tie them all into your argument more clearly. Reflect on ways in which you can apply the concept to the social objects with which your essay is concerned. Often, students fail adequately to link their literature to the question because they do not directly use the concepts and propositions from the literature to understand the objects. Obviously, if you find you do not need the material, it is better simply to delete it.

It is also at this stage that you can think very carefully about the order of the points that you want to make. Each point should develop the argument you are making in an order that makes sense and is intelligible, allowing you to guide the reader through your thinking, to provide evidence for what you are saying where appropriate and then to reach a conclusion that naturally follows from this work. As you think about the order in which you have put your essay together, it can be well worth checking back to the question you have been answering to ask yourself if it runs smoothly. It makes best sense to answer questions in the order that they are posed. In other words, if you are asked to define and evaluate a concept, then you would define it before evaluating it. But this also relates to whatever broader structure you have chosen to use. Thinking about the order in which your points should appear depends upon the decisions you have made when structuring the essay as a whole.

In the 'compare and contrast' structure, for example, we suggested that you generally have to choose whether to compare and contrast element by element, or to make all your comparisons in one section and then all your contrasts in another – and the same kinds of decisions are needed for the other structures discussed. Putting together your argument should be determined by the broad structure and its logic. Some points have to be made before others simply because the later ones depend on them; it would be foolish, never mind cumbersome, to try to evaluate a concept without first having defined it. This is something that has to be worked out each time you write something, for it is context-specific. As a rough guide, however, it can be helpful, on the left side of your argument map, to number each of the points you have made in the order they currently stand. Then, reading through the map of the argument in order, make a further list to the right of each numbered point of all the points that are needed to understand the item in hand. This makes it much easier to see whether you need to rearrange any of them. At the same time it can also be very useful to think about whether you need to say something that you have missed out. When reviewing each point, try to put yourself in the position of someone who has never met the topic before and think about everything they would need to know, not just the points that you have actually made, but to see if there are any you have mentally added without writing them down. Then all you need to do is keep a list of the additional points you need to make and ensure that these get included when you redraft your argument.

This is also the stage when you should do the opposite: check for repetition. In a first draft it is remarkably common to repeat a point you have made. Sometimes this even happens in very quick succession, so that adjacent paragraphs argue the same thing. This can happen when you have tried to make a point but got a bit lost. It might be that in the second paragraph you have tried to have another go at making the same point without fully realising that is what you were doing. Identifying the point being made in each paragraph of your first draft is the only way that you can find these kinds of repetitions. If you find this has happened, it is best to create a new document and begin a brand new paragraph, written in isolation so as to highlight the main point that you are making, now that you are clear about what it is you are trying to argue. To help you, consider separating the material out into the concepts and propositions you wish to use and those you wish to make, to work out exactly how to redraft. Then slot this newly written paragraph back into your main document, removing the repetitious section entirely.

Many students find it helpful to write their entire second draft from scratch rather than editing the first draft. We recommend this, if you have time, since it allows you more purposefully to draft each section, paragraph and sentence in line with the argument you have determined from reviewing the map of your argument. When reading an essay tutors can readily see whether it is a hastily edited first draft or a completely revised second draft. The difference is often apparent in the clarity, or otherwise, with which the argument comes through, as well as in the signposting you have used (see Chapter 4 on middles) and whether these signposts tally with the content. Much like finding your way to a place for the second time, it is far easier to make your argument clearly and to signpost it and evidence it well when you have written one draft and then begin again from scratch, now knowing where you intend to go.

## CHAPTER SUMMARY: MAKING AN ARGUMENT

- A good essay has a clear argument and is structured in order to build the argument, paragraph by paragraph. An argument need not be 'for or against' but can take a number of forms, including (but not limited to) the following possible structures:
  - *Compare and contrast:* examining two or more items, which might be theories, arguments, journal articles, sets of data and so on. It is important that you use this structure to discern both how the items are similar and how they are different from each other.
  - *Build and refine:* selecting from among a variety of theories, arguments and sources of evidence, in order to gradually build a strong argument which addresses the question in detail. It is important that you use this structure to build a coherent picture, which progresses sequentially towards a vigorous defence of your argument.
  - *The author and their critics:* focusing on one academic's particular theory or approach, in order to examine how it has been used, modified or rejected by other researchers, evaluating its status in the field to which it belongs and sometimes also its relevance to a given issue. It is important that you use this structure to evaluate the theory in light of the broader literature rather than simply putting forward a 'for or against' type of argument.
  - *Data interpretation and analysis:* critically exploring data in order to generate findings and conduct an analysis of these findings, and building towards an understanding of what the data can tell you within its limitations. In such a structure it is important that you remain critical of the data, making sure that you interrogate how they were produced, what their limitations are and examining whether there are alternative possible interpretations of them.
- To build your own argument it is helpful to keep in mind the tools you might use to work with the objects, concepts, propositions and evidence found in your critical reading of the literature:

- *Defining and exemplifying objects and concepts:* using examples, citations and quotations to provide details about the sociological phenomena you are writing about, how they have been examined and how you will approach them.
- *Connecting concepts:* drawing together the concepts from a given text, or from across multiple texts, in order to explain how they fit together, compare or contrast with each other.
- *Identifying connections between concepts and propositions:* showing how an academic argument links concepts and objects into propositions and explaining how key propositions make up the backbone of the argument.
- *Connecting concepts and propositions into your argument:* using, refining and challenging the way in which academic researchers make their arguments directly in relation to the question that you are answering.
- *Comparing and contrasting propositions:* showing that there are similarities and differences between arguments in the literature by virtue of the way concepts and propositions are used, evaluating these similarities and differences in relation to your own argument and synthesising this critical review into a coherent conclusion.
- Redrafting your argument is crucial to ensure that your essay is shaped by the argument you are making, rather than the other way around. When redrafting you should remove material which does not serve the argument you have built and add any necessary material to explain and justify the key steps made in your argument.

## ⊰ 3 ⊱

# BEGINNINGS IN DETAIL

The beginning of an essay should introduce us, much like a short story, to the cast of characters and to the subject matter to be addressed. In other words, the beginning, made up of the opening paragraph or two, should tell us who and what this essay is about, possibly including the major theorists and theories to be examined, and should indicate the areas of sociology and the social world to be considered. In addition, the introduction should invoke the concepts that will be explored in the essay and give readers an idea of how they relate to the theorists and areas of social life under discussion. The beginning of an essay must outline what the argument of the essay is going to be.

Having an argument that runs throughout is crucial to the essay's coherence and success. So, indicating what the argument is going to be right at the beginning is essential. And it should include presenting the structure of the essay. In other words, you should give some indication of the order of the main points you will make and how they fit together. The beginning also needs to state what the ultimate conclusion will be. By doing this, the opening paragraph instructs your reader – likely to be the person marking your essay – in how to approach the text as they read through it. It provides a sense of the reason for being told something, of where the essay is going next and where it will end up. This helps them to see how the argument is going to be developed and to hold in mind all of the points that you proceed to make.

In order to present the outline of the argument at the beginning of your essay, you will already need to have a very good idea of how the argument is structured. When preparing to write an essay you might develop a finely detailed plan of your essay's structure and how the argument will proceed. This is possible if you have done a lot of preparatory reading, note taking and planning. In that case you might follow your plan carefully and so implement it exactly. In these circumstances writing your introduction as the first thing you do in your essay is probably well advised since you already have a clear idea of where the argument is going.

Much of the time, however, many of us are rather less well prepared and instead have to draft the beginning paragraph knowing that it may well require substantial revision depending on the shape of the essay once the whole thing is written. So, by and large, you should expect to revise your opening paragraphs in light of the way the essay has turned out once you have done a first draft. Actually writing the first draft, even when there is a good plan in place, can even be an important part of working out what your argument is, or at least helping to decide the best way of making whatever argument you have already sketched out. If you are writing your essay with less of a plan in place and you are still working out your argument as you write, then it is very important indeed to remember, once you have written the first draft, to go back and rewrite your introduction to make sure that it exactly reflects the argument you have ended up making.

Whichever way you work, there are some important considerations to think about when determining what to include in your introduction and how to organise it. So, whether you are writing your beginning with a clear understanding of what you intend to argue, or rewriting it after producing a first draft of the whole essay, it is most important to think carefully about how to use your opening paragraphs to set out what your argument looks like.

## CONTEXTUALISING THE QUESTION

A sensible strategy that students commonly use in their opening paragraphs is to say something about the broader context of the essay question in order to interest or even provoke the reader. This contextualising strategy can be a very effective way of showing the reader why the question is pertinent and of drawing the reader's attention to the critical features of the question. However, it can also be a significant waste of words if it is not done properly. So take care to cut out irrelevant details in opening paragraphs, otherwise the beginning ends up rambling and doing a needlessly bad job of showing whoever is marking the work what is going to be argued. In order to contextualise your question well, therefore, you should ensure that any details you provide are tailored to the argument that you will be making. Below are three possible ways in which you might provide appropriate context to your question.

1. *Providing some basic numerical data:* This can help to show the preva-lence (or otherwise) of the phenomenon under consideration. For example, the opening paragraph of an answer to an essay question about racism in football could usefully include some fig-ures about attitudes to ethnic differences from the British Social Attitudes Survey. These data might help you to show that racism persists in Britain. Whilst the figures may not be about football directly, they serve to contextualise the issue of racism in football against broader patterns of racism in society at large. This would help you to show that the question about football is relevant to wider social issues and, for example, would help you to make an argument that linked racism in football to more general patterns of racism. In this way you can tie statistical data into your opening paragraphs, directly relating them to the question you have been asked and to the argument you will make.

2. *Locating the theorists or theories within a broader body of academic scholar-ship:* For example, an answer to a question about Jean Baudrillard's theory of consumerism might benefit from some contextualisation in the broader body of academic scholarship on postmodernism and post-structuralism. This would help you show how a critical engagement with Baudrillard's theory of consumerism could be informed by an understanding of the wider critical and cultural project of which he formed a part. It is important, however, when providing such context that you do not distract readers with too much information. When you locate theorists within broader bod-ies of work keep uppermost in your mind that your purpose is to highlight their particular approach and to *link* this to your own argument.

3. *Giving a sense of purpose:* Some essays are clearly about a topic that is of political, ethical or other public significance. For example, you might be asked a question about gender inequality, which contin-ues to be a substantial problem in contemporary British society and elsewhere. Moreover, academic research on gender equality is often about trying to understand how inequalities come about in order to be able to challenge them and thus find a remedy. The scholarship has a clear political purpose. This type of work could provide a valuable context when beginning an answer to a question about gender inequalities in housework in the UK. You might write, for example, that scholarship on housework forms an important part of the broader political project of feminism, and

so may valuably be understood in this context. This would help to show that there are political motivations leading scholars to write about housework and so would help you to frame a critical argument about gender inequality in relation to their research.

These are just some of the ways in which you might provide a context for your questions. But it is important to remember, whatever technique you use to contextualise your question, to do it in order to shed light on how your argument will provide a response to the question. Although they can often be useful, opening paragraphs that provide lots of context can waste words and be distracting unless they are clearly organised to portray your main argument. In other words, you must ensure that the beginning is always tailored to the specific kind of essay you are writing. One or two of these three elements might therefore feature more prominently than others depending upon the kind of essay you are producing.

## FRAMING THE QUESTION

Some essay questions are very specific, allowing little room to shape the way you will approach them. For example, an essay title might ask you to: 'Explain Giddens' version of the individualisation thesis, commenting on his concept of the pure relationship.' This question is quite tightly focused and asks you to demonstrate your skills of sociological understanding and description. Yet even here there is still some room for you to explain exactly how you will interpret the question and which way will approach it. By contrast, essay questions in sociology often offer a broader territory in which students are expected to shape their own approach – and thus their own argument – in their response to the question. This gives you scope to frame the question in the way you choose, using it to link clearly to the argument that you go on to make. For example, you are more likely to be asked to: 'Critically evaluate Giddens' version of the individualisation thesis.' Questions as broad as this become more common as you progress through a degree in sociology or a related discipline because they need more skill and greater thought to produce an answer and require you to demonstrate analytical and evaluative skills. So it is often important for your opening paragraphs to specify your own way of framing the question to reflect decisions you have made as to your own distinctive approach to it. The following question from a course on the 'Sociology of Human–Animal Relations' is an example of one which leaves room for you to make decisions about the way to present your argument: 'How might the human–animal relations observable in pet-keeping be understood sociologically? Consider different approaches.' The question directs you to a specific topic in the sociology of human–animal relations, namely 'pet-keeping', and then asks you to review various approaches to it. In this respect, students are free to decide which approaches to choose and thus how to frame the answer. This freedom means that it is even more important for the beginning paragraph to give an indication of the different approaches that you have chosen to consider, adding, perhaps, why you have chosen these rather than any others.

Many essay questions in sociology will require you to make a choice such as this about which kinds of theories or approaches you are going to use. This is because most topics you are likely to meet have been studied from a range of perspectives on social organisation and human life (for example, some theories prioritise human agency over structure, whereas others are far more concerned with structure) and by use of different kinds of methods (for example, using fixed-choice questionnaires or open-ended interviews). It is worthwhile thinking about the kinds of theories and approaches you will use because your selection will provide different kinds of descriptions of the phenomena being considered and make for a different argument.

Of course, it might be that the approaches you choose are, mostly, those that you feel most comfortable describing, analysing and evaluating. However, there are some additional considerations to bear in mind when deciding on approaches to use in your essays so that you are not just relying on your sense of comfort or discomfort. You need to develop ways of thinking about your work as well as reflecting on how it makes you feel. Making these decisions leads on to working out how to structure your argument, which we deal with more extensively in the following chapters. However, they are also relevant to the beginning of your essay since, as we have said, you should indicate right at the start how you have interpreted the question and how you will respond to it.

When writing about how you will frame and respond to the question you should link your choices directly to the question at hand. For example, in your response to the question posed above about pet-keeping, you would be wise to make sure you indicate which approaches you have chosen to use in thinking about human–animal relations in the context of pet-keeping and to present some reason for having made that selection. Pointing to these choices also helps in mapping out the path you will take through the argument and thus helps the readers to anticipate where you will lead them.

Here are a few examples from sociology students' essays that show how they have tried to frame the questions that have been posed in their essays. For now, we have just taken excerpts from their opening paragraphs to illustrate this particular feature. Towards the end of this chapter we will work through some complete examples of opening paragraphs.

*Essay question: How might the human–animal relations observable in pet-keeping be understood sociologically? Consider different approaches.*

**Excerpt from the essay's first paragraph:**

In this essay I shall be exploring and analysing different sociological approaches in the understanding of human-animal relations observable in pet-keeping, including theories of: anthropocentrism and anthropomorphism; symbolic interaction; and the relation to wider social factors, such as those of capitalism and the commodification of non-human animals/pets.

In this example you can see how the student draws attention to the three sociological approaches or themes that he will be using to explore pet-keeping. This helps him to direct the reader's attention to these features and so to the way he has framed the question posed in the essay. A lecturer marking this assessment would then bear this in mind when reading and assessing the essay. For example, they would check to see whether the student had actually covered each of these three areas. So it is important not only to indicate how you will approach the questions in your beginning paragraphs with reference to the choices you have made, but also then to make sure you do what you have promised. There are too many instances of students referring to themes, theorists or approaches in the beginning paragraphs that do not figure in their argument. So when redrafting your essay's beginning it is very important to check not only that it indicates how you have chosen to approach the question and that this is then reflected in your argument right the way through, but also that you do not include things in your opening paragraphs that disappear from your essay's argument.

*Essay question: Were 1970s feminists right to see marriage and children as oppressing women?*

**Excerpt from essay's first paragraph:**

This essay examines the arguments of two structural conflict feminist theorists: Firestone and Delphy. These theories will be evaluated in the context of modern women's experiences of marriage and having children.

In this example you can see that the student has indicated which theorists will be used in the essay in order to limit his scope of interest. The question is deliberately broad, and asks about '1970s feminists' in order to allow students to make their own decisions about which particular theorists whose work they will discuss. The student states that he will evaluate Firestone and Delphy's work on marriage and having children in the context of 'modern women's experiences'. This points the reader to a particular time frame in which the question of oppression will be considered. It might have been even more instructive to specify what he means by 'modern women', especially if he plans to draw a distinction between the experience of women in the 1970s and contemporary women's experience in the 2010s as being important to his evaluation of Firestone and Delphy's research. In this way, the student could have framed the question even more appropriately by ensuring that the way he wrote his opening paragraph linked directly to the structure of his argument.

Each of these examples shows that it is useful to indicate how you will frame the question in terms of the topics and theorists you will be using to make your argument. It narrows the focus of your essay and helps you not to waffle or try to squeeze in too many topics. In the process it also helps the reader to see how your argument is going to be pieced together in the rest of the essay.

## PROVIDING A GUIDE TO THE ARGUMENT

In order to help the reader navigate their way through your essay's argument it is a good idea to include a guide. This sort of guide to an argument can often take the form of a brief overview of the steps that you will take as you proceed through your argument and reach a conclusion.

This applies whether the essay is based just on a discussion of theoretical materials or on empirical data only, or some combination of the two.

Creating a guide to the path you will take has to be done once you have finished drafting and redrafting your essay. For most of us, this is because it is only at this stage that it becomes possible to say for sure exactly what the order of your argument is and how it all fits together. And even if a detailed and finalised plan is already in place before beginning, it is always worth double-checking in case there has been some shift. As a result, you often have to write a draft of your essay to provide a basis for deciding how the argument will be structured in detail so that then you can redraft the essay more accurately to fit this structure. We deal with this process of drafting and redrafting in more detail in later chapters. But it is worth remembering that since you are likely to know only at the end of your work quite how you pieced your own argument together, you can see that it is best to write the guide to your essay's argument at the very end of all the stages. Indeed, it may well be that it is the very last thing that you write before checking your references, proof-reading and submitting your work.

One way to create the guide to the argument is to go through your final draft and to highlight three types of place in the text: where you have summarised the points you have been making; where you have connected your paragraphs together; and where you have drawn conclusions – all elements which should form important parts of some of your paragraphs. In this way you can see the main steps in your own argument. Then all you have to do is to summarise them in a clear and concise way to tell your reader exactly what you will argue and in what order.

Of course, you do not want to write a replica of the argument in the beginning by putting in lots of definitions, quotations and other detail. Doing so simply risks writing out the essay all over again. So, to avoid merely repeating yourself, you need to find a way of summarising the argument's steps quickly – much like giving someone directions for getting across town to wherever they want to go. Doing that usually means giving someone only the main elements of the journey, just 'signposting' the landmarks that will help them get a sense that they are on the right path. So you say: 'Follow Derby Road until you see the large white church and then turn left.' You do not say: 'Follow Derby Road, which is made of tarmac and has quite a few potholes and once was called London Road and is where I had a minor bump not long ago because of a reckless joy-rider …' In this metaphor, the roads correspond to the main lines of argument and the landmarks to the concepts you will be using in those lines. In other words, you should be directing the reader on the journey of your argument by only showing them the highlights. So it might be appropriate to include very short definitions, limited quotations and biographical details, but only to the extent that these are necessary to providing context (as discussed above) and/or to guiding the reader through your argument's steps.

Below are some of the main techniques you can use in providing a guide to your argument.

1. *Indicate the direction of the argument by introducing the central concepts to be evaluated.*

   This means setting out the main concepts and propositions that will be dealt with and perhaps including a very short definition of the concepts. But remember that the introduction is not the proper place to describe a concept in detail; such work is better saved for the middle of the essay. You might, however, want to indicate which scholars are responsible for the development of particular propositions or concepts. Remember to do so briefly, for this is not the place to present an unduly detailed biography of the scholars you are dealing with. A little background is nice, but it is unlikely that a detailed study of the personal life of your chosen sociological figure will be central to your argument, and so, however interesting, it should not appear in the guide.

2. *Link the argument and central concepts directly to the question posed.*

   Make sure that you show exactly why these concepts, propositions, ideas and thinkers are central to the essay by linking them directly to terms in the question. Also, you must make sure that your guide to the argument links together all the elements in the question. It is all too common to answer only some parts of a question. Making sure there is a good fit between your beginning paragraph and every element in a question is a good way to judge quickly if you have adequately answered each part of it. Some people even highlight or write out each element separately to help make sure none is omitted.

3. *Identify what data you will be using and where they come from.*

   It is a good idea to introduce the source of your data in the beginning of your essay, especially if the data form the bulk of the way you build your argument – and this applies no matter whether the data are qualitative or quantitative. For example, if you are dealing with data from the British Social Attitudes Survey then you should indicate this source, provide a reference and – since the Survey is conducted annually – make it clear which years of data you will be using. Similarly, if you are going to be using qualitative data then you should give an indication of what this comprises (ethnographic interviews, observations, etc.) and how those interviewed were selected. If you are not including empirical data then simply say so – for purely conceptual or theoretical essays are common in sociology. The important tip is to make sure that the question does not require the use of some data.

4. *Indicate the weighting of the elements to be considered.*

It can greatly help the reader if you use sensibly chosen phrases to indicate the major elements of your argument, such as: 'this essay is primarily concerned with …', 'much of the argument will address …', 'the investigation will chiefly consider …', 'three central points will be evaluated …', 'in answering the question, the main issue to be explored will be …', and so on. And, for any issues that do not form the bulk of the argument but are still worth mentioning, you can say: 'this essay will also briefly assess …', 'an important starting point is …', 'I note that …', 'the essay comments on X but then goes on to focus on the main concern with Y …', etc.

5. *State what conclusion you have reached and give some indication of how this is achieved.*

Be clear about what you ultimately argue. For example, if your conclusion is that one particular theory is more appropriate to the study of a given phenomenon than another then you should say so. Of course, you should already have made sure that your conclusion follows naturally from the argument you develop, but it is also important to make sure that this makes sense in the introduction. Make it clear to the reader how the path you will take in your argument does indeed lead to your conclusion. This will help the reader feel that they are in safe hands and, knowing where you are going, they will be able to spot more clearly the way you have made this argument as they read through it. This will make it easier to award you the marks that you deserve. In other words, if you have told them what to look for it will be easier for them to find it.

You can probably see how some of these elements may not be relevant to all essays. For example, in an essay on crime statistics it may not be appropriate to list the major scholars you will deal with because it is the data (and the statistical analysis) that form the primary focus of your essay and basis of your argument. As such, it would be much wiser to spend your valuable words in the first couple of paragraphs describing how you have made use of data in the essay. By contrast, in an essay on one or another theory of consumption or of capitalism it may be far more pertinent to say a little about the theorists whose work you will use. These decisions cannot be made according to a rule and so it is up to you to judge which elements are most appropriate for the essay at hand and on which elements you will place the emphasis.

From these considerations you might be able to see how these elements work and how they might link together. Indeed, using these techniques often involves using a number of them at once. For example, in making an outline of the key concepts used in your argument you might also mention the main scholars with whom you will be in dialogue. The best way to learn how to write a good beginning is to see some of these techniques in action. So make sure to look at some good opening paragraphs from academic journal articles that you are using in your essays, since these will help you to see how scholars working in the field tend to introduce their work. Of course, you are not writing an academic journal article and so your emphasis should be on outlining how you will approach the essay question and making it clear what your argument will be. Looking at student examples can be very helpful in this regard.

## Example 1

*Essay question: Why did Marx think that technology designed to oppress them would 'redound to the benefit of the working class'?*

### Opening paragraph of the student's essay

Marx's account of the role of technology and machines in his theory of history provides what is a paradoxical view of how new technology serves as a tool for both undermining the labour force, and, conversely, a tool for social change which can liberate the labour force from the 'shackles' of the capitalist mode of production. While believing that the deployment of new technology in the capitalist mode of production would serve to displace human workers and prove to be overwhelmingly detrimental to working-class life, Marx also developed the notion that such technology would eventually redound to the benefit of the working-class in the sense that the machines would become established as one of the 'ultimate causal agents for a new form of political society.' (Wendling, 2009) In this essay I will be exploring this seemingly paradoxical account of the role of technology, with a particular focus on the revolutionary potential of technologies that could lead to the proletarian revolution that Marx predicted would arise from capitalist society. [Quotation from a third-year sociology student's essay on Marx's theory of technology, 168 words]

## Strengths

This student articulates the way he has interpreted the question. He identifies the primary concern of the question as being the apparent paradox in Marx's account of technology and its effects on the dialectic between the working class and the bourgeoisie. The student then relates this primary element of the question to the way he plans to approach it. He identifies the essay's focus as the potential of technology to help to bring about the proletarian revolution. Through this the student orients the first paragraph directly to the propositions and concepts put forward in the question.

In this way, the student also identifies his main answer to the question by suggesting that technologies might possess such revolutionary potential. He does so by bringing in a quotation that proposes that technologies could be one of the main causal agents in a revolution. So the student has addressed the question of how Marx thought technology would redound to the benefit of the working class. As a result, the student gives the reader an idea of the way he proposes to answer the question (by focusing on the revolutionary potential of technology) and then indicates what the answer will be (technologies could be one of the major causal factors in bringing about the revolution).

## Weaknesses

Although the student provides some direction about his approach to the question, he does not provide enough in terms of a guide to the argument. Although the reader knows that the student will argue that technologies could have revolutionary potential, it is not clear exactly *how* this conclusion will be reached or in what way technologies could have such a potential. Since the student has done a good job of showing how he will approach the question, only a little more information is needed to indicate what steps he will take to make the argument. This beginning paragraph could be improved simply by adding a sentence or two to this effect.

## How to improve Example 1

In order to see how a guide to the argument for this essay could be provided, some sense is needed as to the way this student answered the question. His essay goes on to outline how technology poses a threat to the working class, since it displaces their labour. But he then turns the essay towards its primary target about *the way* technologies which have had this effect might end up contributing to the proletariat revolution. The student outlines how Marx theorised the relationship between technologies and the project of capital accumulation. He reports that Marx thought that technologies would dissolve the need for a skilled workforce and so render them unemployed, unable to subsist and thus unable to purchase the goods on which capital accumulation depends. As the essay's argument continues, the student also points to a critique of this position which is developed by Marcuse, and suggests a sort of paradox that whilst technologies could bring about a revolution, they also represent a mechanism through which revolutionary thought may be suppressed, for example via the technologies enabling the mass media. This argument allows the student ultimately to conclude that for technologies to have a revolutionary effect there will have to be simultaneous changes to social organisation so that working-class people can unite. In this way he shows that the two elements of technology and social change cannot be separated.

Out of interest, there are some other strengths to this essay that we can discern from having looked at the structure of the argument. We can see that this student has constructed a 'build and refine' structure to the argument, in which he builds the case for Marx's theory, provides a critique from Marcuse and then refines Marx's theory in light of that critique. It is also an excellent example of how to make constructive use of counter-arguments, because Marcuse's critique (the counter-argument) helps to produce the student's conclusion rather than undermine it.

So, how can this framework be used to create a guide to the argument? The key is to identify the main turns in the argument. The student first identifies how technologies could be used to displace labour, then argues that this very displacement might bring about the end of capital accumulation. The student then provides a critique of this position by showing that technologies can also be used to suppress revolutionary thought and so concludes that although technologies have revolutionary potential, such a revolution can only be brought about if social relations are simultaneously changed. This would make for an excellent guide and would provide us with a clear statement about the final conclusion. Here is a way this could be written and added to the student's work:

> First I show how Marx argued that technology could be detrimental to the working class by displacing their labour and then argue that Marx saw that this very displacement could bring about a revolution by undoing the process of capital accumulation. Then I provide a critique of Marx's position, developed by Marcuse, and argue that technologies can also be used to help suppress revolutionary thought. This allows me to conclude that for technologies to have revolutionary effects they must be developed hand-in-hand with changes in working class collective organization. [89 words]

## Example 2

*Essay question: To what extent has new media empowered the individual?*

### Opening paragraph from the student's essay

The constant development and reinvention of technology in contemporary society has provided the world with new ways of accessing media, and the forms of media have seen dramatic changes over the past couple of decades, which has changed the way in which we interact with and produce media. Since the advent of Web 2.0 and social networking sites such as Facebook and Twitter, the world of new media and the internet has become a dominant force in society, with over 2 billion people around the world who have access to the internet, which is over a third of the world's population. With access to new media materials, it has been suggested that media audiences have been empowered by new media in ways which traditional media never could, for example, enabling individuals to take part in political campaigns, or simply being able to provide feedback about what products they want to consume. However, due to issues such as the digital divide, not all individuals may share the same sense of new media empowerment. [Quotation from a second-year sociology student's essay on new media, 172 words]

### Strengths

The student has given some context to the statement about new media and empowerment as posed in the question. In particular she has shown why the question is pertinent, by providing a little detail on the contemporary dynamics of internet use. This links directly to the argument that she goes on to make regarding the empowerment of people through new media. In this way the contextualisation of the question is pertinent, clear and thus works well.

The student has also provided some indication of how she proposes to respond to the question by relating some of the ways in which new media may be seen to empower individuals (political campaigns, consumer choice and feedback) and a way in which it may not (the digital divide). In this respect the student introduces a few concepts, including 'consumer choice' and the 'digital divide'. The student also makes use of a proposition by mentioning that there might be a way in which new media can empower people that traditional media cannot.

### Weaknesses

Whilst the student has given some indication of the way she will approach the question by mentioning some of the ways in which new media may or may not empower individuals, she has not done this as well as she might. A little bit more framing of this information is needed to make it really clear to the reader whether or not this forms the basis of the response to the question. Part of the difficulty is that the student has not provided a guide to the argument, and so the reader does not get a clear sense of the way she intends to make her case about the empowerment of individuals through new media.

Finally, the student does not provide a clear indication of what the conclusion will be and how her argument supports it. Without that endpoint, readers cannot easily make sense of why they are being told what they are being told, making it hard to assess how relevant the material is until the end of the essay – which either might be too late, leaving readers with an unduly negative impression, or might make them re-read in order to check, which is not likely to impress them greatly either.

Remember that this is important because it is just the sort of thing a lecturer marking an essay will consider.

## How to improve Example 2

Although she does not say so plainly, the student does in fact draw on political campaigns and consumer choice as two topics to evidence how new media have helped to empower some individuals. Significantly, she draws on the UK riots in 2011 as an example of the way new media were used to organise people during these events. However, she does not mention this in the opening paragraph, which, given how strongly it features in the essay, she should have done. In addition, whilst the student indicates that there is a problem of the 'digital divide', she fails to explain what this is and how it relates to the question. The concept, as she only explains later in the essay, is relevant because it is about how some people have access to new media and can choose whether to enthusiastically adopt it or to ignore it, whereas others do not have access and thus have no choice in whether to use it or not. The student should have explained this a little at the beginning simply because it figures as her main counter-point in the essay to explain the way in which new media may not empower everyone. It is in this respect that the concept of the digital divide is a crucial part of the path through the argument. To remedy this means revising the sentences in which the student indicates how she will respond to the question so that she outlines the path of the argument more clearly.

In the final paragraph the student states that the essay has shown how new media can empower individuals to a certain degree, through increased autonomy, freedom of expression and the ability to take part in political campaigns. But she points out that, at the same time, it remains important to recognise that not everyone has access to new media. Moreover, she adds, new media may also empower the mass professional media at least as much as the individual consumer, possibly more. It is these points that could valuably be added to the beginning paragraph so that readers know in advance what the student is to argue.

Here are a few sentences that the student has used at the end of her opening paragraph:

> With access to new media materials, it has been suggested that media audiences have been empowered by new media in ways which traditional media never could, for example, enabling individuals to take part in political campaigns, or simply being able to provide feedback

about what products they want to consume. However, due to issues such as the digital divide, not all individuals may share the same sense of new media empowerment. [71 words]

These can be reworked to include the improvements that we have suggested regarding the addition of a guide to the argument in order to provide an indication of what the conclusion to the argument will look like:

With access to new media materials, it has been suggested that media audiences have been empowered by new media in ways which traditional media never could. In this essay I review the arguments that new media has enabled individuals to take part in political campaigns, to organise during events such as the UK riots in 2011, and to provide feedback about what products they want to consume. However, I also show that not all individuals have equal access to new media, producing the so-called digital divide, and so not all individuals may share the same sense of new media empowerment. Moreover, I contend that new media may also empower the traditional professional mass media as well. In conclusion I argue that new media can be empowering to the individual but that it remains important that there are existing inequalities in access and power regarding media communications. [146 words]

---

### CHAPTER SUMMARY: BEGINNINGS IN DETAIL

- The beginning of your essays should set the scene for the argument that you will make in your essay. In order to achieve this, you should choose from a range of techniques, including:
  - providing some basic numerical data about the phenomenon you are writing about, for example, regarding its scale or frequency of occurrence;
  - locating the main theory or theorist you are writing about within the broader sociological field to which their work belongs;
  - giving a sense of the purpose of your essay or of the material you are dealing with, for example, regarding its importance for politics, ethics, justice, public policy and so forth.

- Sometimes it is useful to begin an essay by 'framing the question', especially if the question you have been set is broad and gives you room to interpret it. Framing the question means telling the reader how you will approach the issue, what your focus will be and what kinds of examples you will be using.
- In the first paragraph or two, it is almost always important to provide a guide to the argument that you will be making in your essay, which will mean doing some of the following things:
  - indicating the main concepts you will be addressing;
  - linking your argument directly to the question you are answering;
  - identifying any sources of data you will draw upon;
  - indicating the weight of the elements you will be considering;
  - stating the ultimate conclusion that you reach.

# ⊁ 4 ⊰

# MIDDLES IN DETAIL

The middle of your essay is where the argument is fleshed out, point by point, and the majority of the evidence provided. To understand this, we can recollect what happens in a court of law. Both sides, the prosecution and the defence, do all they can by argument and reason, and by presentation, examination and discussion of the evidence, to persuade the magistrate, judge or jury that their side is the one to be believed. If you are a barrister in the court it is all very well to assert that the defendant is guilty or innocent, but without evidence for either position it is unlikely that you will convince anybody.

In a similar fashion, you need to convince not just yourself but also your reader of the position you have adopted or the interpretation you favour. You will be pitting your own argument against other possible interpretations of the question and literatures on which you draw. It is particularly important to remember that the path you take to reach your conclusions is just as important as the conclusions themselves. Moreover, that path needs to be made plain to the reader in order to make sure that they understand your argument and so evaluate it appropriately.

The evidence you have selected from the mass of materials you will have encountered in your critical reading must be deployed in the way you construct the paragraphs and sentences that make up your essay. You can think of each paragraph as a building block for presenting your case, as though you were in a courtroom, to a reader whom you must assume does not know anything about the issue at hand (even though of course they do). Paragraph by paragraph you should weave the evidence together, presenting your own deductions, comparisons, contrasts, insights and so forth.

Using evidence in the way we have just described is one of the distinguishing features of scholarly work and represents an implicit claim to authority of a very particular kind. In key respects, journal articles, research reports and books published in sociology represent authors' answers to their readers' unspoken questions, such as 'how do you know?', 'why should I accept what you say?' or 'why is your interpretation superior to someone else's?'. This applies just as much at undergraduate level, where your essays must represent answers to your tutors' questions. Thinking about how your essays answer these implicit questions is a central element in the way tutors assess what and how much students have learned about sociological research on the topics that they are studying.

Evidence is crucial. You will find it is integral to each of the broad structures that we reviewed in Chapter 2, 'Making an argument'. In a compare and contrast structure, for example, you may wish to propose that there are similarities between two theories, but you must then go on to explain what the similarities are and provide evidence for them.

## PROVIDING EVIDENCE

Evidence often comes in the form of quotations from the materials you have read, notes made during your critical review of the literature and data that you or someone else has collected. We will deal with how you can use evidence in the form of raw data in more detail in Chapter 8, 'Writing a dissertation'. In this chapter we focus on how you can put quotations from the academic literature to work for your argument.

In order to flesh out the argument, you need to think about which sources you will use from your critical reading and which quotations from those sources you will put to work. This can be done by piecing together the concepts and propositions from your review of this material and the notes you have made. Bringing together different source materials is how you evidence the reading you have done, show that you understand those materials, demonstrate that you can make use of arguments in existing scholarship and synthesise all of this in order to construct your own position in response to the question. These are some of the most important skills on which you are being assessed when you write an essay.

Distinguishing between the published material you present and your own commentary on it is the central issue here. Great care is needed to make clear what part of your essay is reporting what someone else has written and what part is your own critical discussion of what they have written. In order to do so you must use the conventions for quotation, which we detail in the next section. You must also reference your sources using the appropriate citation format, which for sociologists in the UK tends to be the Harvard referencing system. This is important in order not only to provide evidence but also to avoid plagiarism.

There are two ways of referring to academic work you want to discuss. One is to use your own words to summarise what you have read, to 'paraphrase' it. The other is to quote verbatim, using the exact words used in the source. There are various ways in which to do each of these.

In the following example the student makes an assertion about whiteness studies originating in America, an assertion that is not hers but rather one she has discovered in an academic source. Accordingly, she cites the source and adds the page number on which the assertion can be found. She then moves on to cite other sources in which scholars have argued for an extension of whiteness studies into Europe. In this latter case the student is not referring to a specific assertion on a particular page but rather to the overall argument made in those instances in the literature, and, as such, she does not need to indicate a page number.

> The collection of writings which are now being referred to as a discipline under the heading of 'whiteness studies' originated in America (Bonnett, 2008: 189), although recent authors have argued the case for studying 'whiteness' in Europe too (Byrne, 2006 and Garner, 2007).

Further on in the essay the student summarises an argument made by an academic (Jenkins), in one of his publications that she has read. Since the summary of the argument refers to a selection of pages from the source, she obviously cannot quote in full and so a judicious summary is appropriate. Importantly, the student has cited the exact pages she is summarising from the source.

> However, Jenkins has illustrated how difficult it is to establish that 'whiteness' is legitimate, using the example of Wales which is perceived to be homogeneous, although historically Wales was a 'plural' society (2008: 33–37).

However, you can see that the student has separated the name of the author, Jenkins, from the cited year and page of the particular source material, which appears in brackets at the end of the sentence. This is sometimes acceptable, but mistakes can often be made when doing so and it can be confusing for the reader. It can often introduce an ambiguity as to who said what. To be safe, we would recommend that, in general, you avoid placing the name of the author separately from the source. We would revise the above example thus:

> However, Jenkins (2008: 33–37) has illustrated how difficult it is to establish that 'whiteness' is legitimate, using the example of Wales which is perceived to be homogeneous, although historically, Wales was a 'plural' society.

You could also revise the wording and move the author's name:

> However, research has illustrated how difficult it is to establish that 'whiteness' is legitimate, for example using the case of Wales, which is perceived to be homogeneous, although historically, Wales was a 'plural' society (Jenkins, 2008: 33–37).

When using a direct quotation it is also vital to include the page numbers. In the example below the student uses a citation before a quotation to indicate exactly where the words she has quoted can be found in the source by including the page number.

> Garner (2007: 48) describes a norm as 'a practice or an idea viewed as constituting what is normal, in a given place, at a given time, among a group of people'.

Finally, in the following excerpt from the student's work she has quoted at length directly from a source. When quoting more than one or two lines of text it is important to indent the material to help the reader more easily identify the end of the author's words and the return of your own.

> The consequences of white people being the cultural norm are explained by Dyer (1997: 9):
>> White people create the dominant images of the world and don't quite see that they thus construct the world in their own image; white people set standards of humanity by which they are bound to succeed and others bound to fail.

The function of the norm of race in constructing such a world allows those who deviate from the norm to be labelled as different.

In the example above (which is, of course, also indented here to make it easy for you to spot the quotation from her essay), you should be able to see how the student indicates the source and page number and indents the material so that her own words that follow are clearly delineated.

The effect of verbatim (i.e. exact, word-for-word) quotation, whether such selections are short and in line with the text or longer and indented, is to underline the importance of the quotation in the case that you are building. In the last example the student quoted the source verbatim and extensively to highlight some of the important connections made by Dyer between concepts and propositions having to do with whiteness and cultural norms. She then followed this quotation with her own interpretation of the material to advance her argument further. Indeed, this efficacious use of a quotation and some follow-up points is a good example of how to provide evidence and put sources to work.

There is one last style of quotation that is worth mentioning. This is to place a quotation as an epigraph right at the very beginning of your essay or dissertation. An epigraph is generally a short quotation which very succinctly conveys the theme or gist of what is to come in the essay, article or book chapter. Below are the essay question, epigraph and first paragraph of the same student's essay on whiteness.

*Essay question: Critically assess the contribution of the notion of 'whiteness' to socio-logical discussions of race, racism and ethnicity.*

> 'White society hates to hear anybody, especially a black man, talk about the crime the white man has perpetrated on the black man' (Malcolm X, 2001: 484).
> At the height of the civil rights movement in America, Malcolm X was particularly vocal about discrimination against black individuals; his ideas for resolution were to support segregation from white oppressors and institutions.

Reading through the question, epigraph and opening lines one after another gives the reader a sharp sense of the approach the student has chosen to take in answering the question. The use of an epigraph can be a potent opening technique for your essays, but you must make sure to do so sensibly and not so frequently that your tutors become immune to their effect. Used sparingly epigraphs can heighten the coherence of your argument; used too frequently they can obscure what you are trying say. Moreover, it is worth remembering that your tutors must often read over a hundred essays on the same question and might tire of seeing epigraph after epigraph.

## PUTTING QUOTATIONS AND SOURCES TO WORK

As we have discussed, it is important to bring evidence into your essays in appropriate ways. It is then vital that you make use of this evidence. Too frequently students hope that the citations and quotations they include in their essays will speak for themselves. This is not the case. Your tutors will expect you to make use of evidence by integrating it into your argument in one way or another.

The most straightforward and common way in which to do so is to cite academic materials to indicate the source of evidence for assertions that you make. An assertion is something that you state as fact. We saw this in the previous example from a student's essay on whiteness. It can also be seen in the following quotation from a student essay on animal studies. Here the student has made a statement and then backed it up by citing several sources. She has also included the page numbers in those sources on which this specific claim can be found.

> Human interaction with animals has become a central feature of contemporary social life. However the interaction between human and animals has largely been ignored by the social sciences (Sanders, 2006: 2; Noske, 1990: 66; Bryant, 1979: 399).

This kind of citation of academic material provides evidence for claims that you wish to make. It is common to use this technique in order to summarise an argument made in a body of literature by putting the argument into your own words and then citing the appropriate sources.

In order to make the most use of this way of providing evidence, you must ensure that the points that you make immediately afterwards connect naturally and further develop your argument. Here is how the student integrated this point into her essay:

> The new field of Human–Animal Studies (HAS), which emerged in the mid-1990s, was thus based on the need to understand animals as cultural beings rather than as mere cultural products (Joseph, 2010).

In this way the student develops her argument with reference to further academic literature to explain that the field of Human–Animal Studies developed in order to address this gap in the social sciences. Thus she integrates the academic material into her argument.

In the following example a student was asked to 'Critically assess the claim that friends are the new "families of choice" (Weeks *et al.*, 2001)'. The quotation comes from the middle of the student's essay, after he has argued that scholarship has demonstrated the increasing importance of friendships in contemporary British society. The student uses a direct quotation along with summaries in his own words based on the notes he has made on the scholarly literature.

> Whilst it is clear that friendship is an increasingly important relationship in many people's lives, the adage 'you can choose your friends but not your family' may not be entirely true. Allan (1996: 100) argues that 'friendships are not freely chosen. They are developed and sustained in the wider framework of people's lives,' referring to social factors such as location, workplace and even ethnicity which can lead to people becoming friends. In addition it is important to note that friendships can be one-sided and may not be reciprocated by one party, and can represent bad experiences in some cases (Davies, 2011: 82). [Quotation from a second-year sociology student's essay]

This paragraph moves the student's argument forward by introducing a new proposition in the first sentence, namely that friendships are not necessarily chosen in the way we tend to think. The student cites a source in the academic literature and provides a direct quotation. Following the end of the direct quotation he goes on to summarise in his own words the rest of the argument made in the academic source. He ends his paragraph by summarising a related argument from Davies regarding the possibility that friendships sometimes represent bad experiences, with the implication that these are obviously not something that people would choose. The student thus makes use of the quotation and his own summaries of the materials he has read (appropriately cited) to provide evidence for the point that he introduces in the first sentence. In this way the student stitches together material from his critical review of the literature into his own argument. This is perhaps the most common way in which students develop their arguments with reference to scholarly materials.

This is a good example of student work. However, it could be improved slightly by making explicit how the concepts and propositions that are being developed in the academic literature link to the argument that the student wants to make in response to the question. He can sign-post the way this use of evidence develops his argument rather better than he does. It is very nearly clear to the reader, but the addition of just one sentence spells out how he wants the quotation and summary he provides of Allan's (1996) work to relate to the question he is answering. In the same fashion, he could also tie the final sentence, the summary of Davies' work, into the argument more explicitly. Here is our suggested revision of the paragraph:

> Whilst it is clear that friendship is an increasingly important relationship in many people's lives, the adage 'you can choose your friends but not your family' may not be entirely true. Allan (1996: 100) argues that 'friendships are not freely chosen. They are developed and sustained in the wider framework of people's lives,' referring to social factors such as location, workplace and even ethnicity which can lead to people becoming friends. *Allan thus argues that the choice of friends might be shaped by factors not immediately within the individual's control, challenging the distinction of friend and family relationships on the basis of choice.* In addition it is important to note that friendships can be one-sided and may not be reciprocated by one party, and can represent bad experiences in some cases (Davies, 2011: 82). *As such, friendships much like family relationships might be sustained against one's wishes.*

In adding these two sentences (italicised to highlight them) we have helped to make explicit the relationship between the academic literature and the argument that the student wishes to develop in his essay. We have put the evidence to far better use by signposting its relationship to the argument, an issue we explore in more detail below. The key change that we have made is to explain how the concepts and propositions from the literature link to the question that has been posed. The next paragraph in the student's essay goes on to argue that family relationships sometimes work like friendships. In this way, we have helped to make the contrast and comparison between friendships and family more explicit, which, in turn, will help to produce a better conclusion. This kind of work takes control of the material and puts it to work for your argument. Indeed, making explicit the logical connections between the evidence you provide and the question you are answering is crucial to making sure that you present your own argument and not merely the arguments you find in the literature.

## PARAGRAPHS AND SENTENCES

In the Introduction we argued that essay writing means thinking not only about the content but also about how to communicate that content. In turn, conveying what you want to say does not just require constructing an argument, providing evidence or making sure your punctuation does not mislead; it also requires attending to the organisation and coherence of the essay or dissertation overall. While this links back to the discussion in Chapter 2 about the choice of structure for each essay, here the focus is more literally on the way the whole piece is organised. So before even starting to think about sentences and paragraphs, a little attention must be paid to the general question of dividing a piece of writing into parts or sections.

A book is conventionally divided into chapters, as is, typically, a PhD thesis as well as an undergraduate dissertation (the latter can vary between 5,000 and 12,000 words). Deciding whether to divide shorter pieces of writing into sections depends on its total length. A brief essay of 1,500–2000 words is unlikely to need much, if anything, in the way of sub-division, but one of 5,000 words could well benefit from three or even four sections. Even so, an undergraduate essay or term paper does not have to be split into sub-sections or sub-divisions. The work done by sub-sections can just as readily be accomplished by thoughtful construction of the paragraphs. But getting that done well may take a bit of practice, so it is worth considering sections for longer essays of 3,000–5,000 words.

When it comes to paragraphs and sentences the main concern is to use each appropriately to convey your subject matter. Distinguishing between the two is summed up in the following simple observation: 'Between one paragraph and another, there is a greater break in the subject than between one sentence and another' (quoted in Partridge, 1963: 223). All the same, some experts in language point out that the sentence is difficult to define. For present purposes, however, just three things need to be said: first, that the sentence is the largest unit usually recognised in discussions of grammar; second, that it needs a main verb (both these points are dealt with in detail later, in Part III). This section is about the third thing, which is that sentences are the basic building blocks of prose. It is also about paragraphs, which, by comparison, are easier to define: blocks of text composed of one or more sentences.

A paragraph's purpose is both to indicate its position in the structure of the argument and overall narrative/story and to provide associated detail about the particular point it is contributing to that story. From this follows the widespread advice that each paragraph should present just one key point and that its first sentence should summarise that point. In principle, following this advice would allow you to cut and paste the first sentence of each paragraph into a new document, which should reveal the outline of your argument in headline form. However, having each paragraph begin with the main point may be unnecessary, or worse, lead to a very wooden and inflexible way of constructing your essay. It is better to put together your paragraphs according to the point they are to make within the essay rather than stick to a rule about structure. As we described in Chapter 2, 'Making an argument', it is helpful later to create a map of your argument by drawing up a list of the main points of each of your paragraphs together with a note of the sources of evidence that you have used. If you wish, you could use these summaries of the main points as the beginnings of some of your paragraphs as you go about revising the draft, remembering that they should not all begin in this fashion.

If, in general, you start a paragraph with a statement of its key point, the remainder of the paragraph should be used to develop that point and to provide supporting evidence and/or some illustration, and some critical development of your argument. To develop this, the bulk of the paragraph, you should work with the techniques that we have explored in Chapter 2. For example, you should consider how to make use of concepts and propositions, connecting them together, providing comparisons and contrasts. You should also make use of the techniques we have detailed in this chapter, by providing evidence and putting it to work. It is important to make sure that each paragraph contributes enough in that it makes a point and develops it in this way. It is equally important to make sure that it does not try to do too much so that you end up with too many points in a paragraph. Separating out the points is a very practical issue and might be boring, but it is crucial for constructing the detail of your argument and ensuring that your essay is easy to read and sets out your points clearly. We return to this issue below as we discuss the 'topic sentences test'.

As you close a paragraph it may sometimes be useful to hint at a further point that arises from the development in the argument it contains. This new point could be made at the end of the paragraph and act as a kind of 'preview' of the way the next paragraph will continue to develop the argument. The next paragraph must then pick up just that new point, perhaps restate it in different words and then proceed to elaborate in similar fashion. Alternatively, a paragraph may have what feels like a 'natural' end, allowing the succeeding paragraph to begin a separate point without needing this sort of 'preview'. Accordingly, that next paragraph may well begin with a word or phrase that lets the reader know it is a new point and explain how it develops the argument being made.

This is part and parcel of connecting paragraphs together. In order to do so you should be thinking about the breaks between them, and where those breaks are to come. Broadsheet news journalists' paragraphs are often noticeably short, frequently consisting of just one sentence. Submitting their copy in such a form can make the sub-editor's job of trimming the piece to fit the space available much quicker and easier. Having an exact number of words is essential when putting a newspaper together where the size of the paper is, among other things, a key constraint on how much can be included (of course, online publishing bypasses this particular constraint, even if others remain).

For essay writing, however, the constraint of a newspaper page is absent. Watching the length of both your sentences and paragraphs is wise. A series of short, simple sentences is often clearer than a single, long, complex one. Read the following example from a student's dissertation just once and ask yourself how easy it is to remember:

> Concepts of meritocracy in the instance of this enquiry will be used to contest definite effects of deprivation in the latter stages of the research to assess whether or not individuals can be said to fail as a result of deprivation and to what extent students can overcome obstacles of deprivation with hard work and determination or whether certain students simply do not have the ability, the role of the school as a means of educational achievement will also bare consideration.
> [Quotation from a third-year sociology student's dissertation]

Apart from noticing the spelling mistake in the final line (bear and bare are homophones, discussed in Part III), you are likely to have found it hard to take all this in. So a good reason for keeping sentences compact is that it puts less of a strain on a reader's memory. In the process, following the grammatical structure is easier and thus the meaning more readily grasped. Even if a long sentence is not particularly complex, one that is composed of several clauses joined together with 'and' can become tiresome to read.

It is a good idea to read what you have written out loud: you might discover that you are left (literally) with no sensible point at which to take a breath, showing you that your sentences are too long. Similarly it can show up either redundancies and needless repetition or make it easier to spot where different points are being confusingly strung together. Reading your draft aloud can also help detect whether your wisely shorter sentences are coming over in abrupt bursts, which may make reading feel uncomfortably disjointed and, worse, risk undermining the sense to be made of them. Although each of your sentences may be grammatically sound and make perfect sense on its own, having nothing to show what links them together and why they appear in that order can leave the reader needlessly bemused. So the way sentences make up a paragraph, what connects them and the words or phrases used to demonstrate and help the reader across the joins, is as important as thinking about how long they are.

Look at the example below, which is a quotation from a student's first paragraph in an essay on terrorism:

> Terrorism is a fundamental contemporary issue that 'exploded' onto the scene following the 9/11 attacks (Fortna, 2011). Since then it has become the subject of intricate analysis determining what causes certain groups to turn to violent tactics. Terrorism is a highly complex phenomenon and previous literature has found little consensus as to what constitutes terrorism (Smelser, 2007; Della Porta, 2008; Gibbs, 1989; Crenshaw 2005; Fortna 2011; Goodwin 2006; Edwards; 2013). As a consequence of its ambiguity I opt out of this debate, as my essay aims to explore the conditions and causes of so-called terrorism; consequently, for the purpose of this analysis, I will sceptically employ this term throughout. This essay will argue that although theories of political violence and terrorism are to a great extent adequate, it is important to fastidiously understand the geographically unique, physical, cultural, political and historical aspects affecting terrorism, which I call the local environment. Consequently, dominant theories of terrorism overlook certain geographical areas (mainly Africa) due to their ethnocentric nature; therefore I call for a greater scope of analysis that ensures an extensive understanding of the local environment. [Quotation from a third-year sociology student's essay]

You can see that his paragraph begins with three short sentences. Then, the sentence beginning 'As a consequence' is somewhat longer, employing a semi-colon to connect two related points. The following sentence is also long and the final one again uses a semi-colon, making for several long sentences in a row. This variation in sentence length makes for a good paragraph. However, the last sentence could more effectively be split in two, removing the semi-colon and restructuring accordingly. Ensuring that you use different lengths of sentences to communicate your points is important in constructing readable paragraphs. The thing is to ensure that your sentences are as long as they need to be in order to make your point and no longer. Sentences that are too long are often so because the point has been lost in the midst of trying to formulate it, thereby making the argument unclear, or because they are being used to make too many points at once. Here is a good example of both of these problems in one sentence:

> In relation to the paradigms of anthropocentrism and anthropomorphism, the dominating discourse of anthropocentrism reflects the notion that humans are separate and to some extent superior over the natural world and nonhuman animals and thus places humans as subjects.

The student is trying to make three related points: (1) that anthropocentrism, the tendency to see humans as being fundamentally distinct from non-human animals, gives humans individuality and subjectivity but treats non-human animals as an undifferentiated mass; (2) this is despite the anthropomorphic tendency to also give animals human qualities; and (3) that anthropocentrism thus generally trumps anthropomorphism when the two come into conflict. The difficulty the student has had can be seen in how she has got a bit lost halfway through the sentence, as it jumps about wildly from point to point and her argument becomes unclear. This is because she is trying to make three points at once. It is therefore important to ensure that each sentence is just as long as it needs to be in order to make one point at a time. Look at long or jumbled sentences in your own writing to try to discern if they might more effectively be split into two or more separate sentences.

Equally, keeping an eye on the length of paragraphs helps. As already indicated, a very useful rule of thumb is to have one main point, its elaboration and supporting evidence per paragraph, and no more. If paragraphs are running to a full, double-spaced page of A4 on the one hand, or they consist of no more than a couple of sentences on the other, they are liable, respectively, to be too long or too short and deserve careful appraisal at the editing stage. Indeed, for many people, either unduly short or overlong paragraphs are useful indicators of a structure or argument that has yet to be properly worked out.

Some academics and tutors argue that a paragraph should never consist of just one sentence, but we think that the following represents the most sensible advice: 'If you can say what you want to say in a single sentence that lacks a direct connection with any other sentence, just stop there and go on to a new paragraph. There's no rule against it. A paragraph can be a single sentence, whether long, short, or middling' (Cutts, 2009: 122). Whatever your decision on this issue, it is wisest to follow the advice of your tutors in each situation. If you find that your tutors respond negatively to your writing paragraphs consisting of one sentence, then it makes sense to adapt your style to their view on the matter. Worrying about sentences and paragraphs in this much detail should, however, be left until writing your second draft, or revising your first draft. It is too much when writing the first draft to focus on details like these, important though they are. Instead you should concentrate on the main task of sorting out what you want to say and getting an initial version of your thoughts down. It then becomes more important, when you come to redraft and edit your work, to keep a careful eye on whether sentences and paragraphs are serving their purposes, or getting too long or short. Indeed, looking first at the length of either is a useful, quick way of easing yourself into the task of editing, checking and revising the first draft.

## TOPIC SENTENCES AND SIGNPOSTING YOUR ARGUMENT

Perhaps the best signposts are those small, but judiciously chosen, words or phrases that help readers to find their way through the text. The obvious main signposts are the essay title itself, which lets readers know broadly what it is about, followed by an introduction which announces the argument and a conclusion that brings it all to a close. In between these two, readers need some thoughtful guidance to help orient themselves as you lead them along your path. It is crucial that the signposts tell readers where you are going in order to make your argument and that they are not merely a list of things that you talk about.

Therefore a prime purpose of the signposting through your text is to signal at successive points where the reader will be going as they move through your argument. This is signposting at an organisational level, making your argument explicit at the key waypoints that you and your reader have reached.

This type of signposting can appear in various guises; adding, building on a previous paragraph or section, providing examples, refining and making a point more precisely, restating an idea or reformulating it to improve clarity, especially when a point is complicated or an idea difficult. Words and phrases that do these different types of signposting for you can easily be spotted. Not only will you notice that authors tend to develop their own collection that is typical of their style, you may already have your own preferred list, which is liable to grow as you read. Adding, for instance, can be signposted with 'as well as' or (obviously!) 'in addition'. Restating or reformulating an idea can be signalled with 'in other words' or 'put another way'. Turning to make a point that contrasts with the preceding one can be foreshadowed with 'conversely' or 'nevertheless'.

In Chapter 2 we examined the use of an argument map in redrafting your essays for your argument. Part of this work consists in taking the main point made in each of your paragraphs and writing them down in order to determine the best sequence for your argument, checking as you go whether you need to add material or to cut it to avoid unnecessary repetition. These sentences are otherwise known as 'topic sentences' – those that summarise the topic of the paragraph. Topic sentences can act as a guide through the argument. As you move from your first draft into a second or final draft you can check whether you have provided enough in the way of topic sentences to lead readers through the argument. In the example below, the student begins his paragraph with a topic sentence.

> Furthermore, new media has been used in a similar fashion to how it was used during the London riots, in that it can be used for political activism. [Quotation from a second-year sociology student's essay]

The student uses a signposting word, 'furthermore', to signal to the reader that the next point develops the argument along the same lines as the previous one. The rest of the paragraph in his essay provides detail about how new media have been used for political activism. Here is another example, this time of a student using the final sentence of a paragraph to summarise the topic:

> Thus, whereas most new social movement scholars advocate a shift away from the Marxist concept of class struggle, it may be argued that an analysis of class struggle is exactly what is missing from the analysis of movements such as Greenpeace. [Quotation from a third-year sociology student's essay]

This sentence summarises the material provided in the paragraph in order to indicate how it relates to the argument and to move the essay on. The first sentence of the next paragraph in the student's essay continued this line of argument by taking Greenpeace as an example.

> In his case study of Greenpeace Canada, John-Henry Harter (2004: 86) beckons[1] for the reinsertion of class analysis into NSM discourse, claiming that to abandon class analysis when studying new social movements is to create a 'false picture of social movements as it renders the actors as being without class interest.' [Quotation from a third-year sociology student's essay]

These two sentences signpost the essay's argument to the reader. Together they indicate that whilst some scholars have argued that alternative theories to class struggle are needed to understand new social movements, others have argued that class might now be missing from work on such movements. The student's point seems to be that the literature is divided on whether class struggle is an important consideration to bear in mind when analysing new social movements. This would make for a concluding signpost, which could be added to the student's essay before moving on to another line of argument. In this respect the student can explicitly state her own argument by using signposts like this to guide the reader from the beginning through to the end of the essay.

---

[1] There is a small vocabulary problem at this point – the use of 'beckons' followed by 'for' is neither correct usage nor does it mean 'call for' or 'plead', which would seem to be what is intended.

Signposting does, however, need a light touch. Certainly obeying the well-worn maxim 'say what you are going to say, say it and then at the end say what you have said' can be especially helpful when giving a talk or a lecture where the audience can only listen in real time. But when the material is written down readers can obviously turn back if they have got lost or need to remind themselves of the shape of the argument. Overdoing signposting to remind readers where they are or what is to come next, and (worse!) doing so in an identical fashion each time, is liable to irritate more than help them. For example, if every paragraph you write ends with 'in the next paragraph I argue …', you will find that readers risk being distracted by this attempt to lead them through the argument instead of being helped. It is much more important that you use the signposts to point to significant turns or developments in the argument. Certainly each paragraph should have a main point, but there is no need for all of them to include an explicit signpost.

Balancing the use of 'however', 'therefore', 'in contrast', 'in addition' and so forth alongside the use of topic sentences and other signposting techniques is a crucial part of drafting and editing. When you work through your initial draft for its first redraft and edit, you may well want to add some signposting. But after taking a break, before going through the essay once again, it is useful to double-check in case some also need removing, modifying or just toning down a bit. You may well discover that the signposting is heavy-handed and was added more for your own benefit when you were still writing to work out your own thinking. Once you have got to the stage when you know what you want to say, you are likely to find you can reduce the frequency of signposting or vary the vocabulary whilst still giving your reader a clear idea of where they have come from and where they will be taken next by referring to the key turns you have identified when using your argument's map.

The most important thing to do with signposting, then, is to guide the reader through the argument, not the essay. Pointing out each turn or move in every paragraph in an essay would be tedious. Instead, point out the key turns and moves in the argument, which will come less frequently than every single paragraph, for it usually takes more than one paragraph to explain and evidence a key point in your argument. Ensuring that you have a good beginning and end, that you clearly articulate where you are going, how you get there and what you have found, will enable you to use signposting in the middle as judiciously as possible and to avoid boring the reader.

## CHAPTER SUMMARY: MIDDLES IN DETAIL

- The middle of the essay is where you must flesh out your argument and provide evidence for your points.
- When providing evidence for your points you must clearly distinguish between material which is your own writing and material which you have paraphrased or quoted by using whichever citation system your institution specifies.
- There are various ways of citing and quoting from academic materials, which you should ensure that you do properly.
- Using a mixture of verbatim quotations and summaries in your own words, etc., helps stop your middle section from becoming formulaic.
- When you provide evidence, whether using citations from academic literature or primary data, you should be sure to explain the evidence and analyse it in order to link it directly to your argument. The evidence cannot be left to speak for itself.
- The middle of your essay should build your argument paragraph by paragraph, and each paragraph should be built sentence by sentence.
- In general, each paragraph should make one key point and no more. Usually paragraphs should consist of more than one sentence, but there is no fixed rule to follow. The important thing is that each paragraph explains the point concisely and provides enough information to make it clear to the reader how the point fits into the argument which is being developed.
- To signal the key points in your argument, it is often helpful to 'signpost' them, for example, by summarising what you have argued so far and what you will go on to argue, or by making explicit how the points raised thus far relate to your broader argument and help answer the question.
- As you redraft your argument it is helpful to pay close attention to the use of 'signposting', ensuring that you provide an adequate guide to your argument as your progress through the essay, but take care not to overdo it.

# 5

# ENDINGS IN DETAIL

Bringing your essay to a close can be the most challenging part of writing. Students often struggle with conclusions, commonly because they are unsure quite what they need to do. It is generally also this part of the essay that is most neglected during a rush to finish the essay. However, the conclusion is just as important to your argument as the beginning and the middle. Imagine if a film or novel started well, but fell flat at the end by failing to make sense of what had happened in the middle. You would be appropriately disappointed and the same is true for your tutors when they assess your work.

For the most part, students use the conclusion to summarise the points they have made in the middle of the essay, and link their conclusions back to the essay question and to the opening paragraphs. While this is essential to producing a good conclusion, it is not enough. It is also reasonably common for students to include some of their own thinking or opinion on the question at hand. This is perfectly acceptable, but it is important that your opinions make some sense in relation to the evidence you have provided and the argument you have developed.

In order to produce a very good conclusion you will need to synthesise the material and evidence for your argument, evaluate the key points you have made, add some of your own thoughts on the matter should you so choose and then provide a firm answer to the question in light of this.

## SYNTHESISING THE ARGUMENT

Providing a summary in the conclusion comes quite naturally to most students and generally takes the form of a quick reminder of the key points that were presented in the middle of the essay. This is fine, but it is much more powerful to synthesise the material and evidence you have provided in order to review your argument. This will allow you to provide a better evaluation of the points you have made and to reach a clear conclusion. Doing so, however, is only possible if you have done enough work in the middle of your essay to construct a sensible argument. In order to demonstrate this and provide a good conclusion, it is worth looking at a number of examples that illustrate how important a strong middle is to the ability to conclude effectively.

If you have not made a clear argument with ample evidence in the middle of your essay it can be easy to fall into the trap of repeating work you have already done when it comes to writing a conclusion. This happens because you are still trying to work out what you want to argue. Worse, you might find yourself adding new material in the conclusion if you have not adequately built an argument in the middle. Below is an example from a student's essay on human–animal relations in which she has tried to summarise the points she has made but instead ended up repeating areas she already covered in the middle of the essay.

> In conclusion, this essay has looked at how animals are understood in reference to the paradigms of anthropocentrism and anthropomorphism. For anthropocentrism animals are perceived as distinct and separate relative to human beings. For the anthropomorphists, animals are attributed with human characteristics such as moods and feelings as seen in pet-owner relationships. Thus this discourse rather than subjugating nature on a hierarchical basis aims to give agency to nonhuman animals. However this discourse has not only been criticised by anthropocentrists, but even anthropomorphists, such as Milton and Taylor, who claim that there is a need to go beyond the conception of simply attributing human characteristics to nonhuman animals and to investigate the actual interaction between humans and animals, and the characteristics of animals. Both discourses are however important when understanding animals since they allow different ways of investigating what animals are relative to human beings. [Quotation from a third-year sociology student's essay]

In this conclusion the student has tried to provide an overview of the main points that she has raised and to conclude that both anthropomorphist and anthropocentrist discourses are important to understanding human–animal relations. And, in order to provide this summary, she has briefly reviewed and explained the concepts on which the essay has focused (anthropomorphism and anthropocentrism). However, this is the technique of defining and exemplifying concepts, which is much more appropriately done in the middle of an essay. Leaving it to the end is too late. In any case, she had already done this work earlier in the essay, so she is repeating herself rather than adding to the argument. Indeed, repeating information already provided in the beginning or middle of the essay is a characteristic feature of someone struggling to write an effective conclusion. If, in your conclusion, you find yourself writing definitions of concepts, providing more examples or introducing new evidence, then use this to 'diagnose' the probability that you have not done enough work in the middle of your essay adequately to develop your argument. The remedy is to go back to the middle of your essay and work out how you can better develop your argument and revise it accordingly.

To write your conclusion you need to synthesise the material and evidence that you have used as a way of summarising and evaluating your argument. To synthesise means to bring things together in such a way as to produce a connected whole, in this case the primary concepts and propositions that you have used. However, it does not mean repeating what you have already said in the middle. The middle of your essay is where you outline the main concepts and propositions used in the academic literature, provide evidence of this, show how they are connected and by doing so present your own argument. It is *your* argument that you must summarise in the conclusion by weaving together the points that you have made based on your use of the academic literature. Again, this can only be done if your middle section is satisfactory.

Below is a further example, from an essay in which students were asked to discuss whether friends are now interchangeable with kin. One particular student has provided a more effective summary of the main concepts and propositions she has used in producing her argument than has the one discussed above. She does not do the work of setting out the definitions and propositions again but instead links together the main turns of her own argument. The conclusion begins by stating her answer to the question and then moves on to provide a quick summary of how she reached this answer:

> In conclusion, this essay argues that friends are interchangeable in contemporary society with kin as valued personal relationships. This essay establishes how through suffusion (Spencer & Pahl, 2006) the

boundaries between friend and kin are no longer mutually exclusive. The domestication of friendship, (Heath, 2004) caused by the decentralisation of the heterosexual couple, is an example of how friends and kin can both act as valued personal relationships in the private realm of the home. Additionally, this essay reviews how people establish their own 'families of choice' (Weston, 1997) prescribing roles of carer and confidant to non-blood relatives. The use of the language of 'family' to describe the roles of members of a person's personal community reflect the value now placed on these relationships, especially for marginalised groups. This essay thus discusses the changing ways of 'doing' kinship and friendship historically to assert that this suffusion of valued relationships is not necessarily a new phenomenon and is also likely to change in the future. It is through these discussions that it has sought to establish that friends are now interchangeable with kin as valued personal relationships. [Quotation from a second-year sociology student's essay]

In this example the student has provided an overview of the main propositions she has reviewed in producing her argument but without repeating that work. The student has not covered everything that she did in the middle of the essay but has instead focused on the key turning points in her argument. Yet she has still fallen short – just – of providing an evaluative synthesis. In order to do so she would have had to indicate why she gave more weight to certain positions when she moved through these key points in her argument, showing why this view and not others should be preferred. However, she was unable to do this because the middle of her essay was not sufficiently thorough, failing to consider counter-points to the main proposition (that friendships are interchangeable with kin). She did not compare and contrast different concepts and propositions and thus could not provide a strong enough argument. In other words, the essay did not adequately explore the way friendships and family might still be quite distinct. As a result, the conclusion, although a good review of the main points made in support of the argument, was unable to present an evaluation of the evidence to reach a well-justified answer to the question.

Below is a much more successful conclusion written by the same student for an essay in which she was asked: 'To what extent did colonialism transform Indian society?'

In conclusion, colonialism did transform Indian society; however, the extent can be exaggerated. This essay establishes how the history of pre-colonial and colonial India is a constructed history. The bias and oversimplification of colonialist writers tends to produce a static pre-colonial India and perfect British India (Pandey, 1990). In addition, this construction of difference is significant in assessing the extent of transformation of the economy. The acceleration of change to the Indian economy as asserted by the colonialists was not a total transformation. Evidence shows the existence of a pre-colonial capitalist economy within India, such as sustained trade links with the Middle East (Alavi, 1989). The creation of the central administration of colonial India does demonstrate a significant transformation of Indian society. The creation of surveys allowed for the construction of social categories which centralised authority and power for the British administration (Fuller, 1989; Cohn, 1996). Finally, the abolition of Sati by the colonial government represents a change in women's rights within colonial India (Mani, 1987). However, the failure to include women within official discourses helps to explain why in contemporary Indian society women's rights have been so slow to progress and transform. Therefore, this essay establishes that while colonialist interactions within India did establish change in the economy, administration, and social organisation of India, the extent of the transformation described in colonialist literature is over simplified and exaggerated by the colonial power. [Quotation from a third-year sociology student's essay]

In writing this essay the student considered evidence that supports the idea that colonialism transformed Indian society, and with it also considered the counter-point by reviewing evidence that shows that claims of transformation may be inaccurate and exaggerated. In this regard she responded appropriately to the question, which concerned the extent of transformation. So the middle of her essay builds up a good argument. As a result, she has then been able to provide a conclusion that does not merely repeat techniques of argument that should be used in the middle, but instead offers a good synthesis of the main turns of her argument and the evidence she has used. Moreover, she has evaluated this material, weighing up the evidence of transformation in India against the evidence to the contrary, to show how she has reached a conclusion to the question.

## ANSWERING THE QUESTION

Concluding an essay by providing an answer to the question is the most important part of bringing it all to an end. However, this does not always mean answering with an emphatic yes or no. Sometimes you will find that you do wish to answer a question by deciding in favour of one or other perspective on the matter at hand, for example, as the student did in the conclusion quoted earlier: 'In conclusion, this essay argues that friends are interchangeable in contemporary society with kin as valued personal relationships.'

You may, however, wish to answer a question with a more nuanced and less one-sided conclusion. Questions in sociology commonly expect you to engage in a critical reading of the literature, to weigh up one position against another and to look for evidence to support these positions. This can often lead to a quite complicated outcome, where some parts of the essay support one position, theory or interpretation, whereas other parts support another. For example, in the conclusion quoted below the student has sought to answer the question 'Does social media empower the individual?', but has found that his critical examination of the literature did not provide a 'yes or no' answer. This is reflected in his much more nuanced summary of the argument:

> In conclusion, it is evident that new media has empowered the individual to a certain degree, in that we now have the freedom to express our autonomy, and the ability to influence social change. However, it is important to not neglect the fact that new media can also be used to empower the professional mass media, not just the individual. New media has certainly had a significant impact on society over the past couple of decades, however it is still a relatively new field, and therefore the implications of what impact it will have in the future are yet to be discovered. [Quotation from a second-year sociology student's essay]

By bringing together the techniques of synthesising the argument with clearly answering the question, it is possible to provide a subtle conclusion that explains how it has been reached in such a way that the reader can clearly understand the essay's argument and show how this does not resolve into a 'yes or no' position.

Here is another example, this time illustrating a thorough synthesis of the argument and presenting a conclusion which weighs up and evaluates the propositions by referring back to the evidence already provided in the middle of the essay. In the light of all this work, the essay is brought to a clear, sensible conclusion.

> This essay has given a brief account of Rich's (1980) argument that women are forced into heterosexuality due to its institutional nature leading to heterosexuality being a compulsory force. These claims were supported by literature from Jackson (1999) and Jackson and Scott (2010) who agree that heterosexuality is an institution that controls relationships between men and women. Such feminists' ideas regarding heterosexuality have been highly influential within the discipline. None the less, the essay has also shown that other thoughts on the character of heterosexuality are credible. For example, Giddens' (1992) ideas indicate how Rich's (1980) position may be redundant in a time of late modernity where women are able to construct their own biographies. Additionally, the arguments put forward by Dunne (1997) and post-structuralists such as Foucault (1979), demonstrate how Rich's (1980) viewpoints may be seen to be essentialist by ignoring agency and choice in a society where the individual has the ability to create counter-discourse. Overall, the essay can close by maintaining that heterosexuality is not as compulsory today as the time when Rich (1980) was writing. Heterosexuality now needs to be investigated through a fresh lens, suitable to a society more in line with that described by post-structuralist theorists. [Quotation from a second-year sociology student's essay]

In this example the student has come to a clear conclusion and has answered the question with reference to the particular concepts and propositions she has explored in the middle of the essay. She has also evaluated her position in relation to the question and is thus able to provide an answer which follows clearly from the work she has put in.

### CHAPTER SUMMARY: ENDS IN DETAIL

- The conclusion of your essay should include a summary of the main points which make up your argument. This means showing how you arrived at your conclusion and not merely stating these points again.

- You should not be providing definitions of concepts, adding more evidence or introducing new issues in your conclusion. If you find yourself doing so, it generally means that you have not done enough work in the middle of your essay to substantiate your argument.
- The conclusion should bring together the main points covered in your essay in order to answer the question.
- To produce an excellent conclusion you must also try to synthesise the key points in your argument in order to show how and why you reached this conclusion rather than another one, as well as indicating what you now can say in response to the question, which you would not have been able to do had you not made this particular argument in this particular fashion.
- You need to summarise *your* argument, not just the arguments made in the literature with which you have engaged.
- You must make sure to answer the question posed, and that you have covered all of its parts. If you have not done so, the conclusion is not the place to rectify the deficit and you must go back to your middle and rework your argument in order to answer all parts of the question in satisfactory detail.
- Answers to essay questions are sometimes clearly in favour of one position rather than another, but they are frequently more complicated than this. An answer might, for instance, agree with a specific proposition in the literature or theoretical approach but only to a certain extent, or in certain contexts, or for certain purposes. Another might conclude that critiques which have discredited a theory, argument or interpretation of a social phenomenon are misplaced, but that alternative critiques explored in the essay are actually warranted, which leaves the original theory just as discredited but for different reasons. These are only two examples of how an answer to a question could synthesise the overall position you have taken in the essay, bringing together the main points in order to come to a nuanced conclusion. There are many other ways of doing this.

# ❧ 6 ❧

# EDITING AND
# PROOF-READING

Unlike earlier stages of work on an essay which you can go back and forth
between (for instance, reading, taking notes and writing), editing and
proof-reading constitute the final stages of completing a piece of writing.
That, however, is all they have in common, for they are wholly different
tasks requiring contrasting types of reading. Editing refers to the work of
revising and reorganising a piece of work (whether it be a film, photo-
graph, text, etc.) to clarify, amend and shape it to serve the author's purposes as well as possible. So it needs the kind of reading that concentrates
on the content, the way it is expressed, how well it flows and so on. This also
means rewriting as necessary.

Proof-reading is quite different. It derives from the practicalities of
the production of a printed item. Proofs are preliminary printed versions
of a book, journal or whatever. Only a few copies are produced in order
that authors and editors may spot and correct any mistakes and generally check through everything to be sure it is all properly presented and
laid out before it is put into production – hence the term proof-reading
to describe the work involved. This type of reading requires deliberately
avoiding attention to the content in order to focus instead on practical
and often quite fine details, such as the way the text is laid out, concentrating not just on spelling but also punctuation and the typeface, noticing
where a word has been omitted, watching for inconsistencies in the way the
page numbers are presented and much more. In direct contrast to editing,
proof-reading must never involve rewriting.

Editing, then, is about the meaning to be conveyed by the way the
text is written; proof-reading is about the way the text looks.[1] Editing is

---

[1] Note that the way something looks is not only about aesthetics but also conveys
information. The conventions for headings, for instance, of placing them on a line
on their own or putting them in italics, signal that they are not a badly constructed

the very last stage of essay *writing*, whereas proof-reading is the very last stage of the process of production as a whole, the final set of tasks to be done before submitting your essay. Allowing enough time for both stages is essential to the quality of the work – especially its clarity – along with achieving a good mark and, it is worth remembering, personal satisfaction. And when scheduling the work right at the beginning, building in time for editing and proof-reading is most important. In addition, timetabling a break between *writing* the final draft of your essay and *editing* the essay is particularly valuable. The break need only be short – though a couple of days, or even more, can often be very well worthwhile. Putting the work aside and doing something completely different, whether or not it is other work, means you return to the final editing and proof-reading refreshed. Everyone can get tired of a piece they are writing, however enjoyable the work has been and no matter how interesting the topic. Equally, working hard on writing something can leave anyone not just tired, but unduly bound up in it, too close to be able easily to see it as others who are new to it will read it. The extra time you leave between finishing writing and beginning editing will help you to read the text in the way your tutor will.

As the final stage of writing, editing ensures that you have converted what up until now may have mostly been a piece of work you have written for yourself, into one rewritten for your readers. This is when you check whether you have redrafted sufficiently to get your argument straight. In redrafting you should have checked whether it all flows well, with sentences and paragraphs following clearly on from one another and you have watched out for any gaps that need smoothing over. Now is the time when you work through the signposting to be sure you have neither overdone it – too many 'now the discussion moves to …' – nor underdone it, leaving your reader stranded without sufficient help. This is when you look out for repetition that holds up the argument. For example, you might notice that you have used the same word twice in one sentence or in a pair of adjacent sentences and so decide to replace one of them with a synonym to make it read less jerkily, or you might realise you need to turn a sentence round to make it read more smoothly, for instance changing it from the passive to the active voice.

sentence but a quick, eye-catching announcement of the section placed immediately below them.

Editing is also the stage at which you might want to consider asking a friend to read your work and make comments. This could be done in the gap between finishing writing and beginning editing so that you can use the comments in your editing work. A close university friend – especially one taking a different subject or a sociology student not taking the same module – can often be ideal, a favour you can return by helping them out in the same way with their own written assignments. A friend can tell you whether they can follow the thread of what you have written, understand your argument, grasp how the evidence you have marshalled supports it and then give you invaluable comments on whether it makes sense.

Having someone else help is particularly valuable when proof-reading. An author is familiar with what they want to say; after all, they wrote the text. As a result they very often see what they intended to write, not what they actually wrote. They may not notice that a key word is missing, since they know what they have in mind. Relatives, incidentally, are also often willing helpers. This is particularly useful for a dissertation or anything longer than regular essays since it asks quite a bit of the person reading it.

Proof-reading is obviously a practical set of tasks. It means checking the spelling, punctuation and grammar, typography and layout, as well as noticing if anything was missed at the earlier, editing stage. It makes sense to start by using your word-processing package's spelling and grammar checker, but you will probably have discovered by now that it is not foolproof – so be sure never to rely on it without additional checks. In any case, unless you have carefully amended its dictionary, it can be completely useless for the names of authors and some sociological terminology. More to the point, spelling checkers cannot pick up some common spelling mistakes, particularly homophones – words that sound the same but have different spellings and meanings such as *their*, *they're* and *there*, *lead* and *led*, *where* and *wear*, and *bare* and *bear* (already illustrated) – any more than they can pick up any sensible sentence that is not the one you wanted to write.

There is a set of common grammatical mistakes and problems with punctuation to be considered when proof-reading. In an essay which reports events in the past, for instance, check to see whether the tense is consistent – have you got a mixture of present and past tense, sometimes writing *is*, *does*, *discusses*, but at other times writing *was*, *did*, *discussed*? Is there subject and verb agreement or have you been concentrating on what you want to write and been beguiled by a word in the plural or implying more than one to make a basic grammatical mistake? One of our own mistakes in an earlier version of this chapter included the mistake 'enough time for both are' instead of 'enough time for both is'. Watch out for common typographical mistakes such as *no* instead of *not*, *of* instead of *or*.

When checking the punctuation, keeping the sharpest possible eye out for both misplaced and absent apostrophes is particularly important. As we mention several times in this book, to many people, including academic tutors, using them incorrectly is – rightly or wrongly – taken to be a sign of the writer's ignorance, carelessness or both. And when doing so, refer to the reminders about other punctuation in the appropriate section of Part III of this book.

It is always useful to teach yourself to notice typography and layout. Simply look at each page as if it were a picture, watching out for things that do not match. Be sure that you have used the same font, and if you want to include more than one, be sure they are used consistently and are not distracting to look at. Similarly, be sure that if you do use italic and bold typefaces you are consistent, as well ensuring you do not overdo it. Look at the way you have laid out any headings and, once again, make sure they are consistent. If you have set some in bold and others in italics, check that you have been consistent so that one is used for the headings and the other the sub-headings. Last, it goes without saying that proof-reading also means looking out for missing words and duplicated words.[2] It is especially easy to fail to notice that a word has been written twice, once at the end of one line and again at the beginning of the next.

If you put a judicious amount of time and effort into editing and proof-reading, you will find you can tackle both with more confidence with each essay. You will also start to see for yourself what a difference it makes to the quality of your written work and how it has improved as time goes on. Here in particular are skills which will stand you in very good stead when you graduate.

---

[2] An example of what professional proof-readers know as 'literals', i.e. mistakes in the original manuscript.

## CHAPTER SUMMARY: EDITING AND PROOF-READING

- Editing and proof-reading are two different stages of the essay-writing process.
- In this context, editing refers to the activity of revising and reorganising an essay to clarify and shape the piece so that it fits its purpose, i.e. provides a clear argument which answers the question.
- Editing makes sure that the piece is written in a way which makes good sense to the intended reader. It is best done once you have taken a break from the essay, for example, after a second draft has been produced. A break can help you to look at the text more objectively, but editing also benefits from having a friend or family member read it since they can do so with 'fresh' eyes, without already knowing what you are trying to say and able to focus on what you have actually said instead.
- Proof-reading means checking that the text is laid out correctly, that there are no spelling or grammatical errors, that there are no missing words or word repetitions, and so on. Proof-reading should only happen once you have completely finished editing the text for sense and meaning.
- Having another person help you to proof-read is perhaps even more important than getting help with editing, for it is often very difficult to spot your own mistakes.

# DETAILED CASE STUDIES OF STUDENT EXAMPLES

## CASE STUDY 1: A PARAGRAPH FROM AN ESSAY ON RACE AND ETHNICITY

Extracted from an essay on black feminism, the following paragraph begins to distinguish black feminism from Western feminism as a basis for reviewing contributions that black feminists have made to feminism more generally together with evaluating their strengths and weaknesses. This is an important paragraph because it contains a point that is crucial to the argument about the way black feminists have criticised Western feminists for homogenising gendered experience. The student shows how black feminists have drawn attention to the ways in which being a woman might be experienced differently when race and ethnicity are taken into account.

It is the third paragraph in the essay, the first of the middle section. The first two paragraphs set out the context and provide a guide to the argument. This third paragraph begins the actual task of making the essay's argument. The paragraph is clear, well argued and well evidenced. Below we show the paragraph in its original form and then go on to outline some of the writing and argument techniques that it illustrates.

*The paragraph in its original form*

Black feminists accuse western feminists of being ethnocentric, something Amos and Parmar (1984: 1) term 'imperial feminism.'

Feminism as ethnocentric is 'the assumption of a unity of women's interests on the basis of white experience.' (Anthius and Yuval-Davis, 1992: 71) This form of feminism regards women as experiencing life as one homogenous group, when, in reality, black women may encounter different experiences compared to white women. As Carby (2009: 444) suggests, black women's experiences cannot be captured within one (white) feminist theory as their *her*story involves unique, numerous and varied experiences. This idea of an ethnocentric, essentialist white feminism is summed up by Harris (1990: 585): 'their work, though powerful and brilliant in many ways, relies on what I call gender essentialism – the notion that a unitary, "essential" women's experience can be isolated and described independently of race, class, sexual orientation, and other realities of experience.' [Quotation from a second-year sociology student's essay]

## Good features of the example

### Putting quotations and sources to work

The student's use of quotations and explication is very good since she brings in work from four different sources, yet her paragraph does not feel over-worked or quotation-heavy. This is because she has chosen short quotations that identify key concepts and made sure that they each contribute something different to the argument. Each quotation and citation of a source builds the main point that ethnocentrism is an issue in feminism because white feminists have tended to ignore differences in the experience of gender. The student has also used a mixture of paraphrasing and quoting, which avoids the repetitive feeling that can come from using too many quotations. Most important, she has also made it clear where she is paraphrasing and identifies the specific page of the source, for example in paraphrasing Carby.

### Sequencing sentences

The student has carefully organised the paragraph so that each sentence develops the main topic. The sentences are logically ordered. The first, second and third sentences in the paragraph all build up an explanation of what ethnocentrism is in the context of feminism. The fourth sentence explains why this is important, in that it identifies the issue of ethnocentrism as having implications for the descriptive power of feminist theory more generally. The fifth sentence nicely summarises the main point being made in the paragraph by using a slightly longer quotation.

## Signposting the argument and sticking to the point

The paragraph has one main point to make, it summarises it using a topic sentence and it sticks to it. The first sentence acts as a topic sentence and identifies the main point that the student wishes to make and it is clearly related to the overall argument. It would have been only too easy for her to cram in extra information, for example, about black feminists' accounts of racism in Western feminism, but she has reserved this point and its supporting evidence for the next paragraph. In doing so she has given herself enough space to make her point clearly, back it up with multiple sources and develop it into a rich account. The paragraph also does some good work in connecting concepts such as ethnocentrism, homogeneity and essentialism.

*Improving the example*

There are some great features of writing and argument in this paragraph and it really shows that the student has read a number of sources and has thought about the order of the sources and quotations she uses. The paragraph focuses well on just one specific and important point and does it justice. In all, the paragraph is a strong example, yet it could be improved a little by tidying up the second sentence, and adding one extra technique.

## Identifying propositions in the literature

The second sentence, which begins 'Feminism as ethnocentric', is a little unclear and so it does not quite make the point as well as it could. It is not a terrible sentence and only needs a bit of improvement. What the student wants to say when quoting from Anthius and Yuval-Davis is that black feminists have pointed out that white feminists assume that women's interests are uniform based only on their own white experiences. So she wants to point out that black feminists have made a proposition about Western feminist literature. The second sentence can be rephrased so that it more clearly shows that the student is quoting from the source as a way of providing evidence for this proposition. Here are two different options for rephrasing the sentence;

1. To say that feminism is ethnocentric is to argue that it relies on 'the assumption of a unity of women's interests on the basis of white experience.' (Anthius and Yuval-Davis, 1992: 71)
2. In proposing that feminism is ethnocentric black feminists are arguing that it relies on 'the assumption of a unity of women's interests on the basis of white experience.' (Anthius and Yuval-Davis, 1992: 71)

Both of these options make it clearer for the reader that the student is adding a critical appraisal by identifying propositions. These alternative wordings show that it is the proposition that has been made in the academic literature that the student wishes to highlight. In this way these alternatives make better use of the critical reading the student has obviously done and make it clear how she is using the evidence to create her own argument. The second option is probably more successful in this regard because it very clearly points out how black feminists are constructing an argument based on a particular proposition and thus evidences the student's own argument.

## The paragraph in its reworked form

Black feminists accuse western feminists of being ethnocentric, something Amos and Parmar (1984:1) term 'imperial feminism.' In proposing that feminism is ethnocentric black feminists are arguing that it relies on 'the assumption of a unity of women's interests on the basis of white experience' (Anthius and Yuval-Davis, 1992:71). This form of feminism regards women as experiencing life as one homogenous group, when, in reality, black women may encounter different experiences compared to white women. As Carby (2009:444) suggests, black women's experiences cannot be captured within one (white) feminist theory as their *her*story involves unique, numerous and varied experiences. This idea of an ethnocentric, essentialist white feminism is summed up by Harris (1990:585): 'their work, though powerful and brilliant in many ways, relies on what I call gender essentialism – the notion that a unitary, "essential" women's experience can be isolated and described independently of race, class, sexual orientation, and other realities of experience.' [Reworked quotation from a second-year student's essay]

## CASE STUDY 2: A PARAGRAPH FROM AN ESSAY ON GENDER AND SEXUALITY

The following paragraph comes from an essay on the sociology of gender and sexuality. It forms part of the student's overall argument that heterosexuality is no longer compulsory but remains the dominant norm in social organisation and identity politics. In other words, the student's overall argument is that lesbian, gay, bisexual, trans and queer (LGBTQ) people now have more legitimate identities, for example, in that their sexual practices are no longer illegal, but it is still largely assumed that people are heterosexual and this is widely reflected in social organisation.

The paragraph we have selected is an important one in the student's essay because it acts as a hinge, linking the first major point being made in the essay (that heterosexuality is no longer compulsory) to the second major point (that heterosexuality is still the dominant framework). It is a fine paragraph and illustrates a number of the writing and argument techniques that we have described. However, there is some room for improvement with just a little editing and by using one extra technique.

*The paragraph in its original form*

> Whilst the gains of the liberation movement cannot be ignored they are also not without consequences. As Jackson and Scott (2010: 99) note 'Progress, however, has its price in the heterosexualisation of all relationships.' By this Jackson and Scott mean that same sex relationships are generally more accepted if they fit in with the dominant normative values, such as monogamy, child-rearing and economic individualism. Seidman (2005: 45) explores this idea further, suggesting we now often make use of the concept of the 'normal gay' in thinking about sexuality, this meaning a gay person who is 'presented as fully human, as the psychological and moral equal of the heterosexual.' By integrating the 'normal gay' into the normative organisation of relationships, we lose the power that LGBTQ people might have to challenge heterosexual dominance. This can also create a division within the LGBTQ community, between those who conform and those who do not. This notion has been termed 'heteronormativity', defined by Duggan (2003: 179) as 'a politics that does not contest dominant heteronormative assumptions and institutions, but upholds and sustains them, whilst promising the possibility of a demobilised gay culture anchored

in domesticity and consumption.' [Quotation from a second-year sociology student's essay]

This paragraph comes about halfway through the essay. The point that the paragraph makes is that whilst liberation movements have made political gains, they have lost the power of a radical politics of sexuality (freed from gendered norms and so forth) and have been integrated into heteronormative structures. It adds an important point to the essay, along with a couple of useful concepts (i.e. 'normal gays' and 'heteronormativity').

The paragraph is clearly written, and although it introduces some complicated concepts it explains them clearly and ties them into the developing argument well. The paragraph builds the argument through the use of the concepts it deploys rather than just adding concepts haphazardly. As such, the concepts are being used in service of the argument and it is clear that the student has thought carefully about each sentence.

## Good features of the example

### Sequencing paragraphs

The essay is arguing that heterosexuality is no longer compulsory but is still the dominant normative framework for sexual identity. In the previous paragraphs the student has written about how the LGBTQ liberation movement has made important political gains and opened up a space for LGBTQ identities. The paragraph quoted above thus serves to move the argument on from the first major point being made in the essay (heterosexuality is no longer compulsory) towards the second major point (heterosexuality is still the dominant normative framework). In doing so the paragraph links to the previous paragraphs in the first sentence ('the gains of the liberation movement cannot be ignored') while at the same time opening up the route to the next major point to be made ('they are also not without their consequences'). This is how linking paragraphs works best, in that the sentence helps to move the argument on by introducing a new point that is simultaneously linked to what has come before.

### Providing evidence and putting quotations and sources to work

This first linking sentence is then developed using a short quotation from Jackson and Scott. The quotation follows on from the first sentence by adding the proposition that all relationships have been heterosexualised as the liberation movement has made its gains. Importantly, the student does not just leave this quotation standing on its own in the paragraph. Instead, she expands on the point made by Jackson and Scott and further explicates it using her own language in the following sentence. She paraphrases some of what Jackson and Scott go on to argue in the chapter from which the quotation is taken and so helps the reader to understand the point being made. The student uses a range of techniques for providing evidence and ensures that the evidence she provides is put to work and linked to her argument.

## Connecting concepts

After introducing the idea that all sexual relationships have been heterosexualised, the student goes on to link together two more concepts to expand on this point. She quotes from two further sources to introduce the concepts of the 'normal gay' and 'heteronormativity'. By bringing these two into the paragraph the student has helped to examine the way in which sexual relationships have been heterosexualised. This is a good example of connecting concepts because each of the three concepts linked together (heterosexualisation, normal gays, heteronormativity) build up into a coherent sequence. Each concept adds to and extends the previous concept in order to make the point about heterosexualisation more clearly. The concepts are used to explain the student's argument.

### Improving the example

These are some great techniques of writing and argument in the paragraph. Clearly the student has done some good critical reading in order to bring out the concepts in a controlled and coherent manner. She has spent time making sure to explain the quotations she has used without being repetitive, and to build them into the argument by connecting the concepts. This student must have spent time writing and editing this paragraph to make sure everything linked together and was organised in a sensible manner. However, there is still a little room for improvement and the paragraph could be made even better. With just a small amount of editing the paragraph can be made that much tighter and more clearly organised. At the moment the writing has two defects.

## Too many points in a paragraph

The paragraph tries to do too much. It is already a complicated and important paragraph because it links three concepts together. From analysing the construction of the paragraph so far we can see that 'heterosexualisation', the 'normal gay' and 'heteronormativity' form the main sequence of ideas in the paragraph. These concepts help the student to make the larger overall point in the paragraph. However, in the last line of the last quotation the student has crammed in a bit too much of Duggan's argument, so that the point about domesticity and consumption takes the reader on to a new issue. Certainly it is true that the point follows directly from the main point about heteronormativity, but to understand quite how heteronormativity relates to domesticity and consumption the student would have to provide rather more explanation of the quotation. If she had outlined the relevance of domesticity and consumption, the paragraph might well be stronger in terms of analysis but it would also become much too long and long-winded. Instead, she should have just cut the Duggan quotation off at the point where it reads 'upholds and sustains them'. This would make the quotation link only to the main point about heteronormativity. She could then use the ideas about domesticity and consumption in a following paragraph or, if they risked leading the essay off in an irrelevant (albeit possibly interesting) direction, just cut them out of the argument altogether. The decision about whether to include these ideas and give them further explanation or cut them would have to be made on the basis of how necessary they are to the overall argument. This small change will ensure that the main point to be made in the paragraph is clear to the reader and that it is fixed firmly in the sequence of the argument. The additional text in the quotation leads to too many concepts and wordy sentences that can leave the reader a little confused at the end. Taking care only to quote those parts of the source that you need to evidence your point is important in writing a clear, strongly organised essay which will score high marks.

## Sentences out of order

In making the point that heteronormativity has been one consequence of liberation movements the student wants to argue that this heteronormativity has implications for LGBTQ communities. However, the organisation of the sentences that develop this argument is a little muddled. Fortunately, it can easily be fixed. The sentence that begins 'This can also create a division' is out of place. Instead, it should be moved to follow the quotation from Duggan's work, remembering that the last bit of the quotation is to be cut. That quotation explains what heteronormativity is and helps to move the argument of the paragraph towards dealing with the implications that heteronormativity has for LGBTQ communities.

Finally, we can add one further technique to ensure that this paragraph not only builds on the argument but also clearly demonstrates the way it is doing so.

## Signposting the argument

As already discussed, the technique of signposting helps to build the argument of the essay in an explicit fashion so that what is outlined in the introduction can clearly be seen to play out as the argument unfolds. Not all paragraphs have to include signposting. Instead, signposting the argument is most effectively done when there is a clear turn to be made, a new direction to be taken in moving through the main points of the argument. The paragraph already opens with a good sentence that links together the previous point and paves the way for the next one. However, the end of the paragraph currently just falls straight into the next one. Making matters worse, the next paragraph moves on to a different point about sexual intercourse. And although it undeniably develops the argument, it still means that this paragraph loses the extra impact it could have and which it deserves, given how important it is as a hinge in the two parts of the overall argument. So, the argument made in the paragraph can be quickly summarised and then linked into the broader argument of the essay as a whole. For example, the following sentence could be a useful way to signpost how this paragraph fits into the essay:

> In this way, the liberation movement has perhaps inadvertently helped to produce heteronormativity by seeking legitimacy for LGBTQ identities.

By stitching this new final sentence into the paragraph and making the other revisions suggested, the extract is transformed into a conceptually strong, clearly written paragraph that serves as a coherent contribution to the argument's development.

*The paragraph reworked*

Whilst the gains of the liberation movement cannot be ignored they are also not without their consequences. As Jackson and Scott (2010: 99) note 'Progress, however, has its price in the heterosexualisation of all relationships'. By this Jackson and Scott mean that same sex relationships are generally more accepted if they fit in with the dominant normative heterosexual values, such as monogamy, child-rearing and economic individualism. Seidman (2005: 45) explores this idea further, suggesting we now often make use of the concept of the 'normal gay' in thinking about sexuality, this meaning a gay person who is 'presented as fully human, as the psychological and moral equal of the heterosexual'. By integrating the 'normal gay' into the existing normative organisation of relationships, we lose the power that gay people might have to challenge heterosexual dominance. This notion has been termed 'heteronormativity', defined by Duggan (2003: 179) as 'a politics that does not contest dominant heteronormative assumptions and institutions, but upholds and sustains them'. Heteronormativity can also create a division within the LGBTQ community, between those who conform and those who do not. As such, the liberation movement has perhaps inadvertently helped to produce heteronormativity by seeking legitimacy for LGBTQ identities. [Reworked quotation from a second-year student's essay]

## CASE STUDY 3: A PARAGRAPH FROM AN ESSAY ON SOCIAL THEORY

The following paragraph features in the middle of the argument in an essay on the importance of Foucault's thinking for postmodern scholarship. The work covers a range of topics, including medicine, sexuality and the Panopticon and explores a number of Foucault's concepts, including power, knowledge, discourse and normalisation. It also tries to situate all of this in relation to the question by linking some of these topics and concepts to theories of modernity and the Enlightenment. Overall the essay is reasonably successful but tries to do too much.

The paragraph quoted below introduces Foucault's thinking on the relationship between his concepts of knowledge and power, and exemplifies this by referring to the Panopticon. It forms part of the student's overall argument that Foucault helped to move away from previous understandings of power and knowledge. The paragraph is first presented in its original form followed by an outline of some of the writing and argument techniques that it illustrates.

## The paragraph in its original form

> Perhaps the most important element of Foucault's work, that on Power/Knowledge should now be considered. 'In the modern world, the development of power and knowledge are so intimately interwoven that they cannot properly be spoken of separately.' (Cuff et al 1998, p. 270) Whilst previous conceptions had seen power as something in the hands of individuals or groups such as the ruling class, modern notions suggest that it is 'diffused throughout the affairs and activities of society.' (Cuff et al 1998, p. 270) Foucault develops this analysis in relation to the development of the prison and the emergence of sexuality. In *Discipline and Punish* (1977) Foucault uses the example of the Panopticon as for him it captured 'the essence of the disciplinary society.' (Bartky 1988) The Panopticon is a prison designed by Jeremy Bentham where a circular system of cells surrounds a single guard tower. Each cell has two windows, one facing the windows on the guard tower and the other facing the outside. This has the effect of establishing a backlight so that the prisoner is visible in their cell at all times (Bartky 1988, Elliot 2009, Cuff et al 1998). A 'one way, total surveillance of prisoners by the prison staff' is created (Elliot 2009, p. 73). The outcome is that the prisoner can never definitively know whether or not they are being observed and the theory is that this constant threat modifies behaviour. [Quotation from a first-year sociology student's essay]

## Good features of the example

### Defining and exemplifying concepts

The student has done a reasonably good job of introducing some concepts. He begins by looking at the concepts of power and knowledge and then explores the concept of the Panopticon, as devised by Jeremy Bentham and revised by Foucault. He then goes on to explain what the Panopticon is and provides examples drawn from the literature. As we described in Chapter 4, 'Middles in detail', a definition of a concept should be supported by an academic citation. It also often requires further exemplification to help make full sense of the concept in relation to the essay question being answered. Here the student has cited academic sources where explanations of the Panopticon can be found and which support his summary. He also uses these sources to illustrate the concept with reference to the guard tower, the windows, the lighting and so forth.

## Providing evidence

This paragraph uses two ways of providing evidence. First the student has cited academic sources, as with those used to support his explanation of the concept of the Panopticon. He has also indicated the original source in Foucault's own writing for this concept. Second, he has included some direct quotations from Cuff et al. (1998) and Bartky (1988) and uses these to explain how Foucault conceptualises the relationship between power and knowledge. Importantly, he has remembered to include the page number when he has used a direct quotation.

*Improving the example*

The student has clearly engaged with some scholarly literature in constructing this paragraph and he uses it to define and exemplify some concepts in order to build his argument. How he does this could be improved, however, by making clearer use of the concepts and propositions he brings in from the academic literature and by linking these to his argument in order to answer the question. Whilst the citations and quotations he uses are helpful and do provide evidence for the point he wishes to make in this paragraph, he could have strengthened it by using a direct quotation from Foucault. A quotation is not added to the paragraph here, partly because rewriting the paragraph completely is unnecessary, but partly because the student himself would have needed to do some additional reading. Instead, we will highlight how the paragraph can be improved using the techniques outlined in this book. To make the connections between the question and the literature that he has cited, the student could, for instance, have made use of an additional technique, namely signposting.

## Connecting concepts and propositions in your argument

As it stands, the student uses the literature to introduce some concepts and does some work to identify a central proposition in Foucault's account. The direct quotations from Cuff et al. are used to indicate that Foucault's conception of power and knowledge involves a proposition stating their inseparable relationship. Power always involves knowledge and knowledge power. These quotations are also used to introduce the idea that power is diffuse and not simply concentrated in the hands of the ruling class. To make better use of these concepts and propositions, however, the student could connect them more clearly in his argument.

In order to do so he could add a sentence that explains how this material helps him to answer the question, which is: 'Outline and critically assess Foucault's contribution to postmodern thought.' This paragraph occurs in the middle of his essay and is used primarily to outline a key aspect of Foucault's thinking; as the student says, 'Perhaps the most important element of Foucault's work, that on Power/Knowledge should now be considered.' This sentence is indeed a gesture towards the essay question but it does not go far enough in showing how the whole paragraph helps to answer the question. The point of the paragraph is to outline Foucault's theory of power and knowledge, but not (yet) to assess it critically. That comes later on in the essay. Here, however, he does need to show that this issue has directly to do with postmodernism. Earlier in the essay the student has outlined Foucault's concept of discourse and now he means to add a further set of concepts to show that Foucault contributed a good deal to postmodern thought.

The section of the paragraph with which we are currently dealing consists of the first three sentences. In order to tighten it up, we propose replacing the first sentence of the paragraph with a new one that directly links the concepts and propositions to the question. The new sentence is italicised below:

*Another of Foucault's key contributions to postmodern thought is in how he uses the concepts of power and knowledge, seeing them as being fundamentally connected rather than concentrated in certain parts of society.* 'In the modern world, the development of power and knowledge are so intimately interwoven that they cannot properly be spoken of separately.' (Cuff et al 1998, p. 270) Whilst previous conceptions had seen power as something in the hands of individuals or groups such as the ruling class, modern notions suggest that it is 'diffused throughout the affairs and activities of society.' (Cuff et al 1998, p. 270)

This first sentence helps to make a far clearer connection between the paragraph and the question that the student is answering, paving the way for the evidence for the point to be provided using the quotations that follow.

## Putting quotations and sources to work

In the first few sentences the student uses two direct quotations from Cuff et al. (1998) that provide some explanation of Foucault's concepts of power and knowledge and how they are related. As just indicated, the italicised additional sentence at the beginning of the paragraph helps to frame the quotations from the academic literature that follow. Now they more clearly relate to the question and develop the main point of the paragraph by providing some evidence. So this additional sentence helps the student to use the technique of 'putting quotations and sources to work' much more effectively, as well as to connect the concepts and propositions to the argument. In this way the various techniques themselves link together. Indeed, they can sometimes be accomplished simultaneously, as this case illustrates.

## Editing and redrafting for the argument

Editing is just as crucial as writing, and when editing it is important to revise your work so as to improve the organisation and clarity of your argument. This is the focus of the editing process. In the following two sentences from the middle of the paragraph, the student could improve the clarity of his argument and shorten the paragraph slightly with a little minor editing. We propose condensing the following two sentences:

> Foucault develops this analysis in relation to the development of the prison and the emergence of sexuality. In *Discipline and Punish* (1977) Foucault uses the example of the Panopticon as for him it captured 'the essence of the disciplinary society.' (Bartky 1988)

This is readily done by removing the reference to sexuality, which the student goes on to deal with in a later part of the essay and is in any case better left to that section. The quotation from Bartky's work is moved to the end of the paragraph mainly because the student has not yet discussed disciplinary society. Here it is used to signpost the argument that the student is trying to make as well as making the connection to the paragraph that follows. The way in which the citation to Foucault's work is written is revised to have the year follow the author's name. Finally, the vocabulary is tidied up a little and the order rearranged by bringing some of the first sentence into the middle of the second one. The revised sentence now reads:

> In *Discipline and Punish* Foucault (1977) develops this analysis by reference to the prison system, using the example of the Panopticon.

## Signposting the argument

After introducing the concept of the Panopticon, the student cites a number of sources as he explains what it is and how it works. He does a good job of this and little editing is needed. Moving this reference to Bartky's work to the end of the paragraph will help the student more effectively tie the concept of the Panopticon and its exemplification into the argument. The last sentence will need to be adjusted accordingly. In order to signpost how this paragraph fits into the argument the student needs to make sure that the last sentence relates to the new first sentence that has been produced. The first sentence is now rewritten like this:

> Another of Foucault's key contributions to postmodern thought is in how he uses the concepts of power and knowledge, seeing them as being fundamentally connected rather than concentrated in certain parts of society.

This already does some good work to signpost the argument because it links this paragraph to the question posed. Here is the final sentence as it stands, which comes after the student has explained how the Panopticon functions:

> The outcome is that the prisoner can never definitively know whether or not they are being observed and the theory is that this constant threat modifies behaviour.

The task is to connect the rewritten first sentence to the final one. The last sentence as it currently stands clearly relates to the quotation from Bartky's work about disciplinary society. So this sentence can now be edited and we can add one containing the quotation from Bartky and link it all back to the first sentence, thus:

The outcome is that the prisoner can never definitively know whether or not they are being observed, which creates a power relation with the guards and encourages the prisoners to modify their behaviour. Foucault saw the Panopticon as being 'the essence of the disciplinary society' (Bartky 1988) in which power and knowledge were tied together in this way more generally.

This is now a far stronger ending to the paragraph because it ties the paragraph into the argument. It also now paves the way for the next paragraph, in which the student goes on to discuss Foucault's account of normalisation in the disciplinary society.

## The paragraph in its reworked form

Another of Foucault's key contributions to postmodern thought is in how he uses the concepts of power and knowledge, seeing them as being fundamentally connected rather than concentrated in certain parts of society. 'In the modern world, the development of power and knowledge are so intimately interwoven that they cannot properly be spoken of separately.' (Cuff et al 1998, p. 270) Whilst previous conceptions had seen power as something in the hands of individuals or groups such as the ruling class, modern notions suggest that it is 'diffused throughout the affairs and activities of society.' (Cuff et al 1998, p. 270) In *Discipline and Punish* Foucault (1977) develops this analysis by reference to the prison system, using the example of the Panopticon. The Panopticon is a prison designed by Jeremy Bentham where a circular system of cells surrounds a single guard tower. Each cell has two windows, one facing the windows on the guard tower and the other facing the outside. This has the effect of establishing a backlight so that the prisoner is visible in their cell at all times (Bartky 1988, Elliot 2009, Cuff et al 1998). A 'one way, total surveillance of prisoners by the prison staff' is created (Elliot 2009, p. 73). The outcome is that the prisoner can never definitively know whether or not they are being observed, which creates a power relation with the guards and encourages the prisoners to modify their behaviour. Foucault saw the Panopticon as being 'the essence of the disciplinary society' (Bartky 1988) in which power and knowledge were tied together in this way more generally. [Reworked quotation from a first-year sociology student's essay]

The changes improve the paragraph but they do also increase its length, which was quite considerable already. Since the paragraph now flows quite nicely it is fine either to leave it at this length or to split it in two, at the sentence that begins 'In *Discipline and Punish*'.

In sum, these revisions have cleared up the language a little, more clearly tied the paragraph to the argument that the student wants to make, made it relate directly to the question and improved how well the academic sources have been put to work. This is now a strong paragraph. In the process each sentence had to be checked to be sure it contributes to the main point regarding the proposition that Foucault makes about the way the concepts of power and knowledge should be connected. In order to make your argument effectively, it is thus important to put aside enough time to write a second draft and edit it.

# ⇒ 8 ⇐

# WRITING A DISSERTATION

In many institutions the dissertation is the equivalent of a whole course, and is sometimes optional. Its length is commonly around 10,000 words, perhaps a little more or a little less. There are also degree schemes in which a shorter dissertation, usually of around 6,000 words, is possible. Whatever the length, the dissertation is likely to be the most significant, extended piece of work that you will produce during your time as an undergraduate student. It can certainly represent a challenge to your analytical and creative powers. But it also offers what is probably the first opportunity to employ those powers to explore a topic of your choice in detail and with far fewer constraints on your writing than you will have had before. Unlike your essays, where everyone in your class tends to be working on the same question, when you write a dissertation you are most likely to be examining something very different from anyone else, or even if tackling a similar topic you are liable to be doing so in a completely different way.

The dissertation topic is generally flexible to accommodate your interests. This means that you are likely to be able to choose to write a theoretical piece, or one that reports on secondary data, or that presents your independent collection of primary data of one kind or another. The type of dissertation that you choose to pursue will make a great difference to how you must construct your argument and write up your findings. In one way, much of what you have to do is an extension of the techniques that we have covered in this book so far, from critical reading right through to writing a conclusion. At the same time, however, there are additional ways in which putting together a dissertation is different from writing a shorter piece.

Note that this book does not cover everything that you need to know about conducting your own research and writing a dissertation. There are several other books that deal with this in great detail, specifically concentrating on what is involved in preparing a dissertation. So, as well as working through this chapter, it would also be wise for you to consult such books for advice on conducting research for and managing a dissertation project (a selection is listed in the Appendix).

In this chapter we concentrate on some of the ways in which writing a dissertation builds upon what we hope you have already grasped about essay writing from what we have covered so far. In the process, we also point out some of the important differences between essays and dissertations. We focus on how you can piece together an argument in your dissertation by ensuring that you answer a range of implicit questions that could be posed of your work. But before moving on to any of these, we begin in the next section with the major task of identifying the topic on which you want to work. We focus on this because perhaps the biggest difference between a dissertation and the majority of undergraduate essays revolves around the topic and question to be tackled. By and large, your tutors set the questions on which you are to write your essays. Doing a dissertation requires that you identify the topic and then create your own question(s) – and that highlights the importance of devoting quite a bit of thought and time to this preliminary stage.

## SELECTING A TOPIC, DEVISING A RESEARCH QUESTION AND WORKING TOWARDS ANSWERING IT

Whatever kind of dissertation you write, you must choose a topic that is sociological, meaning that it is informed by debates, concepts and theories from the academic literature. You will be expected to identify not only a topic on which academics have written, but also a specific puzzle or problem, related to this topic and literature, about which you can formulate a research question. This is not to say that you will necessarily start with a ready-made topic that is recognisably sociological, although you might. Instead, you may begin from an issue, activity or problem in the 'real' world which is not yet expressed in sociological terms. So the very first task is highly likely to be working out how to transform or translate your interest into one that is characterised sociologically. This is an especially important stage, which is far too commonly insufficiently well developed.

Responding to the question(s) that you devise should involve significant independent work. This will mean locating and studying a large collection of library materials, possibly drawing on archives or repositories of data, in order to construct a review of the relevant literature, the boundaries of which you must develop for yourself. Devising your own question(s) and finding relevant materials are likely to overlap with each other, involving your moving backwards and forwards between the two types of work – in much the same way that although the stages of writing an essay can be listed in a logical progression one following another, in practice there is a good deal of doubling back and forth.

You will then use the literature, as you would in an essay, to answer the question by informing your own argument. Since you have come up with the question yourself, identified a puzzle related to the topic and identified a set of literature to assist you in your pursuits, you will be heavily engaged in creative work. In other words, you must produce a response to your question that cannot be answered simply by showing how other academics have already answered this question – largely because the chances are that such work has not been done in quite the way you are tackling the topic. You must, if only in a modest way, create a new argument. In order to do this, it is imperative that you select a topic that interests you sufficiently to hold your attention through to the end as well as one on which you can develop an independent and informed view. Similarly, it is always advisable to try to avoid well-worn topics – a matter which is worth exploring with your dissertation supervisor. Year after year, tutors see the same kinds of questions being asked and the same kinds of answers being produced, and they are much more likely to be enthused by something new. As you consider what your topic will be and begin to word your question, it is essential to discuss with your supervisor whether this represents a reasonably novel 'take' on the sociological issue at hand. Novelty is unlikely to be an overarching requirement for an undergraduate dissertation, although at graduate level it is the defining characteristic of the PhD. But for undergraduates, thinking about what you have already learned in a new way, with fresh eyes, to open out a different line of thinking is one of the opportunities offered by doing a dissertation.

To get inspiration for your topic, think about the courses that you have enjoyed and consider asking your course lecturers what kinds of issues are currently being debated in the literature. And, as hinted above, you might initially be inspired by an everyday issue that intrigues you or even by which you have been personally affected or in which you are involved. This can be one route into finding something that enthuses you, but be sure to ask your tutor for help in turning your personal interests or experiences into a proper sociological puzzle. It is also well worth looking for literature that discusses the issue, for sometimes it is a good deal harder to do good work on a topic about which you care personally than one with which you are not immediately associated.

The typical problem that students encounter when formulating a question is that it is too broad, covering too great a range of phenomena or literatures. Gradually narrowing down and refining the overall question and sub-questions should be a deliberate focus at the early stages, but also may well continue throughout the period in which you are working on your dissertation. As you review the literature, conduct any empirical work that might be planned and inspect and analyse your data to turn them into findings, you should reflect on whether your question or sub-questions need to be revised. In exploring the literature in detail, for example, you might see that you need to narrow your question in order to ensure that it is novel or adds something, since some aspects will have already been covered by other researchers. Similarly, in examining your data, you might unearth findings and come to conclusions that do not adequately answer the original question that you posed; in this case recasting the question a little to reflect what you have found more directly is a sensible remedy. If you do end up adjusting your original research question, make sure you include discussion of the way subsequent work led you to do so as part of your presentation of how you went about doing the work – probably in the methodology/methods chapter.

## THE DISSERTATION STRUCTURE

Having begun to establish your sociologically characterised topic and got down to work on developing a suitable research question(s), it is worth becoming familiar with what a dissertation looks like and how it might be structured. Some people find that reading previous students' dissertations offers a useful guide. Others, however, find this makes them nervous and undermines their confidence, leaving them wondering whether they could ever live up to what someone else has accomplished. Make up your own mind as to which sort of person you are, and in the meantime, start to think about how you wish to organise your own dissertation. You do not need to wait until you have formulated your research question(s) before thinking about the way you wish to structure your dissertation. Indeed, doing them in tandem, flipping from one to the other, can be fruitful, helping you to firm up both. Do remember that nothing has to be fixed at this stage, any more than anything needs to be finalised in the early stages of beginning work on an essay. But starting to rough out a structure gives you a basis for revision and improvement as you continue work.

In general your dissertation will include:

1. An introduction that states the research question(s) and discusses how you came to formulate it (them);
2. A review of the literature that outlines the relevant debates, findings, concepts and theories of the field of enquiry in which your research question is located;
3. A methodology that describes the methods used together with a discussion of the underpinning philosophical considerations;
4. Presentation of the findings from any empirical work you undertake;
5. Interpretation and discussion of your results in light of the academic literature you reviewed earlier;
6. A conclusion that brings everything together to make sense of the dissertation as a whole;
7. Any appropriate appendices followed by a list of references.[1]

Each of these elements will be more or less prominent, or may not appear at all, depending on the kind of dissertation you are writing. Clearly you will not have any empirical findings if your dissertation is a theoretical one. Exactly how these parts are structured into chapters and sections is equally, if not more, varied. For example, the presentation of the findings might be collected into one chapter and then discussed in a separate chapter, or the findings and discussion could be done together, but separated into three thematic chapters, each presenting a sub-set of the findings alongside their discussion in light of the literature. These decisions must be made consciously and through reflection on how best to present your data or theoretical material and your discussion. Here too is another aspect which is well worth talking through with your dissertation supervisor as these decisions are often particular to any one combination of the topic, question, literature, methods and findings.

To assist you in writing your dissertation and ensuring that each chapter contributes to the overall argument, it is useful to consider each chapter to be an answer to a number of implicit or unspoken questions that

[1] For definitive details of the order in which what publishers refer to as the parts of a book are put together, see Turabian (2013).

could be asked of your work. In assessing your dissertation your examiners will often have certain of these questions in mind anyway, even if they (or, come to that, your tutors) never utter them out loud. We think it is useful to spell them out, for it helps to understand why a dissertation structure looks as we have sketched it above and gives you more of a thought-through basis for making decisions about the way you want to organise your own. Accordingly, in the following sub-sections we outline the questions that you should in effect be answering by each broadly defined chapter or section and provide some advice, where relevant, on how to draw on and develop further the techniques we have presented in the book.

Before going through each in detail, here, in brief, are the unspoken questions (in italics) for the sections already listed above:

1. An introduction that states the research question(s); *what is this dissertation about?*
2. A review of the literature that outlines the relevant debates, findings, concepts and theories of the field of enquiry in which your research question is located; *has it been done before? if so, how? was it good enough? is it too long ago? are there new approaches that were omitted? etc.*
3. A methodology that describes the methods used together with a discussion of the underpinning philosophical considerations; *what did you do? what was your strategy, i.e. your overall approach? how did you turn that into a distinct, describable set of procedures or methods?*
4. Presentation of the findings from any empirical work; *what did you find out?*
5. Interpretation and discussion of your results in the light of the academic literature you reviewed earlier; *how do you interpret or explain what you found out and why? are there any limitations?*
6. A conclusion that brings everything together to make sense of the dissertation as a whole; *how have you shed light on your original research question(s)? are there any practical or policy implications? what do you want the reader to make of all this, i.e. what is the reader to have learned and understood about your dissertation?*

## The introduction

Much like the introduction to an essay, the introductory chapter of your dissertation should outline the context of your research question, providing the necessary information for the reader to understand why this question has been posed and what wider significance it has for sociologists and people more broadly. Unlike most essays, however, the dissertation introduction must more clearly justify the choice of question. Then, as with an essay, it should outline how you intend to frame the question, approach the argument and what you will ultimately conclude.

The questions implicit in the introduction are:

1. Why have you chosen this topic?
2. Why should someone other than you be interested in this topic?
3. What do we need to know in order to understand the social phenomena that you are researching?
4. What overall research approach and which academic literature(s) will be brought to bear on this topic?
5. What is the specific research question and what are the sub-questions?

Of course, you should not answer these questions as you would in a general conversation. You are unlikely to write that 'People should be interested in this topic because X, Y and Z.' Instead, the answers should be implicit in how you write your introduction. Regarding the first question, for example, you should outline the social significance of the topic, how – or indeed whether – it has been investigated so far and what you will do to remedy any deficiencies in the academic understanding of this topic. Question 2 implies that you should tell your reader something about why this topic is important in the social world, the 'real' world, for 'everyday' people, politicians, industrialists or whomsoever it concerns. Question 3 then asks you to set out the necessary background information for the reader to understand something about the topic. For example, if you are writing about a government policy you should tell your readers when the policy was created, by whom and in what context, and perhaps some information about how it links to other policies. Dealing with question 4, the outline of your approach, you should refer to the main concepts and propositions with which you will be concerned. Note that it is too soon to go into detail about them. At this stage, just sketch them so that your reader can look out for them and know what is coming; detailing these parts of the work is properly reserved for the literature review and the discussion of the findings. Finally, question 5 should be answered explicitly – you must tell your reader very early on exactly what it is you are asking and how you will break this larger question down into smaller questions that can be tied directly to your general approach, the design of your study and the methods that you will use.

Consider the example from a student's first attempt to frame her dissertation question and a couple of her sub-questions:

Main question: How do contemporary integration discourses construct Muslims, Britishness and their relations?

Sub-question 1: How do labels and narratives of radicalisation and community cohesion construct ideas of what it means to be British?

Sub-question 2: In what ways are Muslims constructed in relation to the War on Terror?

In the main question, the student has referred to 'contemporary integration discourses' but has not adequately brought these into the sub-questions so that the sub-questions end up being broader than the main question. Instead, the sub-questions should narrow the focus. She then made some slight adjustments and was able to link them together more effectively:

Sub-question 1: How do labels and narratives of radicalisation and community cohesion construct what it means to be British in the Prevent and Shared Futures policy documents?

Sub-question 2: In what ways are Muslims constructed in relation to the War on Terror in these two policy documents?

These sub-questions are more clearly connected to the main question because they refer to the policy documents that she goes on to use as the basis of her discourse analysis.

### Literature review

In your review of the literature you should be using some of the same techniques that we have outlined in the book so far, including defining objects and concepts and connecting concepts and propositions in order to present an overview of the relevant literature that will help you to answer your research question(s). The implicit questions to be answered by your literature review chapter include:

1. What do we already know about the topic under investigation from the existing academic literature?
2. What approaches and methods have been used to study the topic?

3. Are there any limitations in the literature as it currently stands; if so, what are they?
4. How does your approach complement, extend or contrast with the existing approaches in the literature?

Incidentally, if you are tackling a topic which is also of interest among one or another group, or indeed of current public concern, there is likely to be newspaper coverage as well as other literature on it, reports from think tanks, NGOs and pressure groups and much more. In such circumstances it is even more important than ever to ask yourself all the questions discussed in Chapter 1 on reading critically, to help you identify the genre of whatever you are looking at to distinguish it from academic literature. This is part and parcel of sorting out for yourself the kind of position the authors take on the topic and whether they simply 'push' one particular position or consider alternative points of view and weigh them up to assess their merits, strengths and limitations.

In writing the first draft of your literature review, it is helpful to keep in mind that you will most likely have to revise this draft once you have completed your findings and concluding chapters. The literature review should roughly 'mirror' your later chapters, so that all the themes you go on to explore in your findings are adequately set up and so that you do not introduce a large number of themes that do not later turn out to be useful in your data analysis. Providing an overview of the relevant concepts and propositions from the literature is a way of marshalling your resources for later use when describing, contextualising and evaluating your findings. Much as with an essay, your engagement with the academic literature should provide the tools with which you will construct your dissertation's argument.

## Methodology

The methodology is sometimes overlooked by students in their efforts to get ahead in their work and to move quickly into an analysis of their data. However, the methodology is vital to empirical dissertation projects because it informs readers as to how to view the data, helps them to anticipate the kinds of analysis that will be presented, supports your later reminder of any limitations of your study and thus guides the readers towards an appropriate appreciation of what you have discovered. The implicit questions to answer with your methodology include:

1. How did you go about finding out about the phenomena with which you are concerned?
2. What is the broader philosophical position you are taking? For instance, is it concerned with being objective or does it acknowledge some degree of subjectivity?
3. What particular methods did you use and how did this help you to answer your research question(s)?
4. How did you collect your data, how did you store and analyse them and did you have to take account of any ethical issues at any stage?
5. How did all of this shape your interpretation of the data?
6. What are the strengths and limitations of your approach?

## Findings and discussion

As we have already described, the way in which you present your findings and discussion will differ according to the kind of dissertation you are writing. A theoretical dissertation is likely to present a discussion of key themes in several separate chapters, interrogating the literature, comparing and contrasting different theoretical traditions or inspecting an academic's work, identifying coherences and contradictions and thereby building an argument along the way. Much of what we have covered in the book is directly relevant to such work since it all relies on the way you make use of concepts and propositions, how you evidence your points and connect all of this into your own argument.

In respect of an empirical dissertation, the findings and discussion should present your data in some form or other and interpret them. The data might be represented as quotations from interviews, extracts from field notes or records of observations, statistics, tables, graphs or charts.[2] A mix of such presentations is common, but it is up to you to determine how exactly you will present your data since the decision will

---

[2] Even if you are not presenting numerical data, Chapman and Mahon's (1986) discussion of the basic conventions of presenting tables, charts, graphs is still well worth consulting.

be conditional upon your methodology and how you intend to interpret the findings. Crucially, your presentation and discussion of the findings should be framed by the argument and approach you have been developing in your introduction, literature review and methodology. It is in the discussion of your findings that all of your tools should be brought to bear, to bring out the key dimensions of your data and to show how they can be interpreted so as to help to answer your research question(s). In this regard, the findings and discussion are most like the middle of an essay. As such, it would be wise to consult Chapter 4 of this book, 'Middles in detail', to reflect on the kinds of techniques you should be using in producing evidence for your argument. Some of the implicit questions to answer in your findings chapter include:

1. What exactly did you find? What themes or patterns do your data evidence?
2. Are there inconsistencies or contradictions in your data? What are they and what might these tell you about the topic at hand?
3. How does this information link to the concepts and propositions you have developed in your literature review?
4. What light do these connections shed on the broad arguments and debates in the academic literature?
5. How does all of this help you answer your research question(s)?
6. Why should we be inclined to view your interpretation of these data and your answers to the question more favourably than other possible interpretations and answers?

In order to provide answers to these implicit questions you should make use of the techniques we have outlined in the book so far. The chapters on 'making an argument' and 'middles' (Chapters 2 and 4) should be of particular use, since they provide an overview both of how to use concepts and propositions and of how to provide evidence for your argument. It is important not just to present your findings but also to connect them in your argument. Whether you are writing a dissertation which uses qualitative or quantitative data, the representations of those data should be followed by some interpretation and then followed, in turn, by some explanation of how your interpretation links to the argument you are developing, most commonly by drawing upon the tools you have developed in your review of the academic literature (the concepts, propositions, examples and analogies you have reviewed). Consider the following example from the findings chapter of a student's dissertation which sought to answer the question: 'How do mothers understand and shape their daughter's clothing choices?'

> In support of Woodward's (2007) research, as I proceeded on through the interviews, I uncovered that the mothers tend to see their daughters' style as a representation of themselves, as well as an indicator of their role as a mother. However, when discussing their perceptions of their daughters' friends' style, the mothers had little to say on the matter. Four of the six mothers I interviewed claim not to notice the way their daughters' friends dress. Participant 6 explained:
>
>> I don't know really – I'm not bothered really [with how her daughter's friends dress] as long as my child is neat and tidy I don't care what they wear. I don't want … I make sure she looks good 'coz I don't want people thinking that I, that she's allowed to go out in what she wants 'coz I'm not bothered. She's always well dressed. (Participant 6).
>
>> Here my data corresponds with Miller's belief (1997, cited in Woodward, 2007, p. 104) that infants are initially conceptualised as an extension of the mother. Mothers see their daughters' clothing as a representation of their competence and care as mothers. If the participants are selecting clothes for their daughters which compensate for their dissatisfied style as a child and they view their daughters as a representation of themselves, my data may demonstrate the mothers in part using their daughters to have the identity that they regret not having at their age.

In the example above the student has first reminded the reader about a proposition she outlined in the literature review, and cited the source of the claim (Woodward) before linking this to the data. To substantiate the connection between the literature and her data she provides evidence in the forms of numbers (four of six mothers) and then in the form of a quotation from a semi-structured interview with one of those four mothers. The quotation links to the proposition and the student goes on to further integrate this into her argument after presenting the indented quotation by specifically referring to how mothers view their daughters' clothing as a representation of their competence and care. The second half of the second paragraph, however, then moves on to another point concerning mothers using their daughters' clothing choices to express an identity that they were unable to express when they themselves were children. This second point would need to be evidenced in order for it to be adequately connected into the argument the student is developing. She had not addressed this second point earlier in the dissertation and so there is not enough evidence for the claim that she makes. It might be that the student could develop this point based on findings in the literature (which might well be what she intended by referencing Miller), but she would have to bring in the concepts and propositions from the literature more explicitly.

## The conclusion

The concluding chapter of your dissertation should summarise what the reader is to make of everything that has been presented, from the introduction right through to the findings and discussion. This is your chance to explain what can now be understood about the topic based on the answers you have provided to the questions you posed at the beginning. Much as with the conclusion of an essay, the conclusion of your dissertation should synthesise the key points you have made to provide an overview of your argument, evaluating your position and casting your own work in a critical light.

The questions implicitly asked of you in writing your conclusion include:

1. What have you argued and why should your argument be believed?
2. What are the strengths and limitations of your study and how have you contributed to the literature?
3. Are there any broader lessons to be learned from your study, for example, for social policy, social institutions or industry?
4. What could be done to further develop an understanding of this topic?

## MAKING YOUR DISSERTATION MANAGEABLE

Perhaps the main thing when approaching writing your dissertation is to concentrate on all the separate stages of writing an essay, and then, step by step, work out a plan for enlarging them to the scale needed for your dissertation. If you are used to writing a 3,000-word essay, you will need to work out how to expand everything to

something like three times the length. If, however, that seems daunting, a valuable way of 'taming' it is by identifying chunks of manageable length. Simply write out your provisional chapter structure, put
the total number of words you are to write at the bottom right-hand
side of the page, then divide up the words allowed for each chapter
so that your page looks a bit like a bank statement. The list of chapters corresponds to a list of items of expenditure with the number of
words roughly allocated to it in the right-hand column instead of the
amount you paid for whatever you bought. Using an abbreviated version of the example of the structure we presented above, your page
could look like this:

|  | Words |
|---|---|
| 1. Introduction | 750 |
| 2. Review of the literature | 2,000 |
| 3. Methodology, methods and philosophical considerations | 1,000 |
| 4. Presentation of the findings | 3,000 |
| 5. Interpretation and discussion of results | 2,250 |
| 6. Conclusion | 1,000 |
| Total | 10,000 |

Breaking it up like this makes it seem much more manageable, for
each of the chapters suddenly looks like a short essay of the kind you
are already used to writing. You then treat the organisation of each
chapter in the way you prepare an essay, writing an outline and ensuring that you present its argument in a logical, step-by-step fashion.
Once you have got all the chapters outlined in this way, you can then
link them together in just the same way that you bring together the
elements of any essay. Although this one happens to be on a different
scale, all the principles of essay writing apply, piecing it together as if
it is an oversize essay, checking its structure, making sure that each
element follows in a sensible order, with your argument unfolding as
you go. In this way, you will discover that many of the features you have
been working on when you write essays stand you in good stead when
you come to prepare your dissertation. By the same token, working on
your first extended piece of writing that the dissertation represents will
hone your writing skills for the remaining essays of your undergraduate career.

## CHAPTER SUMMARY: WRITING A DISSERTATION

- Although it is important that any piece of writing you produce reflects your own argument, based on evidence you have brought together, it is utterly essential that this is the case in your dissertation. The dissertation will therefore benefit from use of the same techniques outlined in this book regarding the construction of an argument and the provision of evidence to support it.
- Often you will be required to choose which general form of dissertation you wish to write, selecting from: a theoretical dissertation based predominantly on library study; an empirical dissertation based on analysis of pre-existing data, such as the British Social Attitudes Survey; an empirical dissertation based on analysis of data which you have collected.
- Whatever kind of dissertation you pursue, you must ensure that your topic is sociological, meaning that it is informed by debates, concepts and theories from the academic literature.
- You must make sure that you ask a question which can be answered by use of the theoretical tools and empirical sources (whether primarily quantitative or qualitative data, a mix, or none at all) which you select. A mismatch of question and method is one of the most common mistakes made by students in designing their dissertation projects. Be sure to get advice on this before you embark on your data collection or get deep into your library research.
- The question you ask in your dissertation must be broken down into sub-questions, each of which provides part of an answer to the broader question. Remember that you can generally revise your question and sub-questions right up until your final draft, though it is best to do so in consultation with your dissertation supervisor. Make sure to check that what you have written in your dissertation answers the question you posed. If not, you must either revise the material, or alter the question to better reflect what you have argued.
- The dissertation is generally broken down into sections or chapters, each of which can be thought of as answering an implicit question about your project. The introduction of your

dissertation answers the implicit question: *what is this disserta-tion about?* The literature review responds to the implicit ques-tion: *what has already been said about this topic and how useful is it in answering your question?* The methodology section answers the implicit question: *what did you do and why?* The presentation of your findings and their discussion: *what did you find and what does this mean for the question you posed?* The conclusion: *what should the reader make of all this and what are the implications of hav-ing these specific answers to the question posed?*

- The introduction provides the context to your study and helps the reader to understand why the question you have posed is interesting and sociological.
- The literature review summarises and develops from an over-view of the relevant concepts and propositions from your read-ing. This is a way of marshalling your resources for later use when describing, contextualising and evaluating your findings.
- The methodology can sometimes be overlooked by students but it is important, and a good methodology is essential to empirical projects. It should instruct the reader in the general philosophical position being adopted and explain why this is appropriate to the methods being used and why it is use-ful in answering the question. It should identify the sources of data and how they were collected and what limitations there are on the application of these data to your question. It should review the potential ethical issues which were identi-fied before the work was undertaken and what was done to militate against any foreseeable harm to participants and to the researcher. Sometimes it is also relevant to reflect on ethi-cal issues which arose during the conduct of the research, or which might be posed by the answers you have found to the question you asked.
- The findings and discussion present the data and interpret them in light of the question via use of the set of tools which you collected together in the literature review. These sections should draw out the most important findings from the data, showing what can be discerned from them and what remains unclear. How you present the data will depend upon what kind of dissertation you are writing, and it is vital that you seek

some guidance on this. Where possible look at good examples of other students' dissertations. Remember too that there are always lessons to be learned from the academic literature. If you are doing a qualitative project look at qualitative papers which you admire and try to replicate some of what they have done with their data and how they have linked them to their concepts and propositions.

- The conclusion should tell the reader what contribution this dissertation has made to answering the question posed and why this is important. It should, as with the conclusion of an essay, synthesise the argument to bring you to a position of evaluation of the stance you have taken and cast your own work in a critical light.

# ✺ Part II ✺

# TIPS AND TECHNIQUES

# ❧ 9 ❧

# CHOOSING AN ESSAY QUESTION

In your essay assignments you will normally be given a choice of question(s) that you can answer. So it is wise to think carefully about your selection in order that you can best demonstrate your understanding and skills. When first looking at a list of possible questions you will usually find yourself drawn to one or two in particular. This is likely because you found these topics most appealing or you found them most easy to grasp. Of course you should choose a topic that you find interesting since your enthusiasm will help to carry you through the work involved, and is likely to come over well in your written work. By the same token, however, choosing a topic you do not care about but which you think is easy to answer will also show in your writing, this time to your disadvantage. Whilst the person marking your assignment will not focus on your enthusiasm, it is generally the case that your lack of enthusiasm about a topic will affect the argument that you produce since you are more likely to read widely, think critically, mull over your essay and spend time redrafting your work if you are enthused by the materials with which you are working.

Furthermore, it is well worth exercising some caution in selecting a question that seems easy to answer in comparison to the other options. This is because it might sometimes be deceptively simple. Some questions which look easy are commonly much more difficult to answer well. A broad question might seem more simple because you have more choice in what you write about, but this also requires that you put more work into framing the question, justifying your selections and determining the kind of argument that you will make. If you can bear in mind such considerations when selecting an essay question, you will help yourself to make your selection based on a little more planning. Your first instinct can be a good guide but it is best supplemented with a little reflection.

A sensible way to analyse your choice of essay questions is to return to Chapter 2 in this book and to consider which of the general structures most accurately represents the likely shape of a good answer to each question posed. It might be that one or more of the questions takes the format of a 'compare and contrast' structure, while others are more likely to be of the 'build and refine' type. Thinking about which broad structure is most appropriate can help you to understand why it is appealing or not, or why it seems easier or more difficult to write. This is not to say that you should always select the most appealing kind of structure; you may, for instance, be someone who likes to answer 'compare and contrast' type questions. Rather, it is a good idea to have some variety in the kinds of questions that you answer so that you can challenge yourself and become accustomed to answering a wide range of types.

You will not be able to predict which kinds of questions will be asked in an exam, or on which topics that were covered in your course. So, for example, you might have prepared yourself to respond to two or three topics from the course but find that they are all the sort of question that you have tended to avoid. Putting effort into making yourself accustomed to using different kinds of essay structures outside of exam conditions can help to prepare you for these unseen questions, when your decision as to which to answer is under significantly more time pressure.

# 10

# HOW TO DECIDE
# WHAT TO READ

Scholarly and practical considerations come together from the beginning when selecting what to read. Obviously, in order to read something, you have to get hold of it. That may take some time, for instance: an hour locating three online journal articles; an additional hour following up likely looking references you found listed in those articles; a couple of days before you can get back to follow up additional references you have on the list your tutor gave you; several weeks to get hold of a book in high demand at the library. So it is important to realise that decisions about what to read take place over a period of time rather than being made only at the beginning, once and for all. Of course, it is also important to be sure that as you move through the essay-writing process you reduce the amount of reading you are doing and increase the amount of time you spend writing.

Having a sense of the time it will take to acquire what to read has to be dovetailed with knowing the overall timetable for the essay (which always also has to be set alongside thinking about other commitments that must be fitted in during that period). As we have already noted, making sure you reserve enough time to redraft your essay at least once has to be built in to the total timetable, and that probably means you have to recognise that the period of time available for the bulk of the reading might well be much shorter than it seems at first sight.

Once you have started thinking about the timetable, deciding what to read includes other considerations. Deciding what to begin with is one, and being able to recognise different types of material is another. Throughout, you should be remembering your timetable and making judgements about how much reading is needed in relation to it. Chapter 1 on reading critically suggests that you start by reading widely, but then narrow down to focus more closely on the essay topic.

Begin from the course material, the reading lists provided, recommendations made during lectures and your own lecture notes, along
with any suggestions added in a seminar and anything your tutor may
have advised for a particular essay topic. Think about the essay title as
you check the titles of the books and articles to identify any that match
closely. To help you get a sense of what each item covers, use the abstracts
of journal articles, which are commonly available without having to look
up the complete article. Augment that with checking the 'blurb' on the
backs of books or the dust jacket, for which you probably no longer need
to hold the book in your hand, since publishers typically publish such
paragraphs on their websites. Some people find it helps to make a new
document in which to list items that look promising for the essay – a list
of 'possible things to read'. Start with just a few, and then add to it as you
go. You can keep it up to date as you get under way, making very short
notes on each, perhaps dividing them into those that are essential, those
that are desirable and those that you will read 'only if there is time'. This
can usefully help you keep track of where you are if there are several
other courses claiming your attention simultaneously. Even before you
start reading in earnest, you can very probably mark the most important
items, simply based on your tutor's recommendations and prominence
on the reading list.

Textbooks are valuable at the very early stage of reading because they
typically provide pointers to key contributions on a topic along with relevant references. It is most unlikely, incidentally, that relying only on a
textbook, or even two, will be sufficient for an essay, even in your first
year. Similarly, you must never rely only on websites such as Wikipedia.
Instead, you need to make use of academic sources, journal articles,
books and chapters in edited books. Use a textbook to help you to find
more substantive scholarly sources and be aware that textbooks themselves are not a replacement for reading original sources. Be flexible;
begin reading a little to help you get a sense of the range of angles on
your essay topic, and use that growing sense to help you judge other
items on your list of possible things to read. Checking the bibliographies
in textbooks and key recommended references can help you to identify
the most important items. And sometimes, especially if you are in your
final year or working on reviewing literature for your dissertation, it is
very important indeed to go back to an original source. For example, an
essay on the use of official statistics is likely to be much better informed,
and your understanding dramatically improved, if you have read key
passages of Émile Durkheim's *Suicide*, even if you do not read the whole

book. It is very difficult to do well in a sociology essay if you do not read the 'classics' or original sources for the major themes and ideas in the field.

Distinctions between textbooks and original, even classic, contributions to the discipline are just some that can be made between types of material you could find on a topic. As important is the difference between academic and non-academic sources. Non-academic writing would include, say, a party political manifesto, or a news article by a journalist investigating MPs making inappropriate expenses claims. These materials could certainly feature as data in an academic source, for example in a study of the role of political advisers or of white-collar crime, but they are not academic sources themselves. The difference is between documents which represent data – primary sources – and the academic studies – secondary sources – of those documents which use them as data. It is certainly possible to use a primary source such as a newspaper report to help spark ideas about what to look for in the academic literature, but it cannot be counted as the equivalent of research findings or an authoritative source. You must ensure that you mainly work with academic materials, i.e. secondary sources.

Distinguishing between different types of writing is not always straightforward. Academics sometimes write for newspapers, as journalists, or for other organisations as advisers. They may well undertake research according to high-quality academic criteria, but these materials are unlikely to have been peer-reviewed. This is a crucial factor in determining whether the source counts as an academic one or not, even when written by an academic. It helps to consider a series of features, including asking who the author is – are they, for instance, primarily a journalist or an academic – and looking for information on their expertise – do they have an academic post or does their website describe them as a freelance writer? Consider how they write to detect whether they seem to have an agenda, for example, taking sides on some topic without weighing up the strength of the opposition, or thinking about whether they argue the case for their position or assert it as if it were self-evident. Thinking carefully about such considerations will help you to determine whether you wish to treat the source as a secondary source, i.e. as an academic source, or as a primary source, i.e. as data, say, for your essay or dissertation.

## ✺ 11 ✺

# HOW TO GET PAST WRITER'S BLOCK

Writer's block refers to a sudden inability to write. Some talk about a blank page syndrome, likening it to a type of medical or psychological problem. It often seems to happen to people who write for a living or who are famous, novelists in particular. It is obviously potentially very serious for them, since it threatens their income or reputation or both. Anyone who writes can suffer it, including all of us engaged in academic writing, whether in the first undergraduate year or towards the end of a research career. It is typically temporary, and there are several ways round it.

An extremely common reason for what can feel like writer's block is incomplete preparation. Trying to start writing with no plan or outline may well lead to getting stuck as to what to say. There are two alternative remedies for this. One is to stop trying to write, and return to making the outline clearer. Writing a set of sentences which sum up the main points and adding a clear reminder of the supporting reading for each point is one way to do this. Consider whether the sentences are in a logical order, reorganise them if necessary and then develop each one into a full paragraph. Work paragraph by paragraph, without at first worrying about the way they link up. Continuing in this way leads quite quickly to linking the paragraphs and then finding that the writing has got going again. Returning a little later to the early paragraphs to smooth them out then becomes straightforward.

Another way is to remember that one of the uses of writing is as a way of sorting out your thoughts. So just writing down what you think, or even writing as if you are talking out loud, can readily restart the process of getting words on paper. Some people find that writing a slide presentation for an imaginary audience gets past the block, providing notes on the slides as the outline from which to settle to writing the essay. Others advise switching to another task that is related to the essay or dissertation. Breaking off to check that the list of references is up to date or that the bibliographic details are complete can get round the blockage. This can help you avoid worrying about not getting on with completing the assignment, since you are doing something valuable towards it at the same time as taking a little time off from the actual writing.

Now and then being tired, uncomfortable or simply stiff from sitting for a long time can contribute to feeling unable to write and certainly add to not wanting to. Rather than taking a rest on a sofa with a cup of coffee, or talking to a friend – pleasant as those may be – it is often more productive to avoid switching out of work mode completely and instead get some exercise, but still reflect on the substance of the work rather than trying to write about it. This does not necessarily mean going to the gym for a sweaty workout; a gentle walk for ten to twenty minutes may be just as helpful. Many people find that the rhythm of moving coupled with a feeling that they are letting their head go into some sort of a neutral gear results in a sense that their brain has solved the problem in the background without effort, allowing them to return to their desk ready to write again.

For some people, writer's block is muddled up with a temporary loss of confidence. For them, re-reading an earlier, successfully completed piece of their own writing can be a valuable reminder that they have done it before and so can do it again. Return to an essay you enjoyed writing, or about which your tutor made an encouraging remark. See if you can recollect why you enjoyed it or what it was your tutor praised and ponder on what you could do to transfer those positive features to the writing on which you temporarily feel stuck. For other people, reading a book you think is bad or an article which you think misses the point can be immensely reassuring. They find that writing down what they consider is wrong with it reminds them that they have some worthwhile ideas, which in turn gets them writing again, simultaneously restoring their self-confidence.

Finally, it is always worth remembering that an essay can be put together in any order. Indeed, it often works best to assemble it from the middle outwards, as it were. Starting in the middle, beginning by writing a section which will have to go in somewhere, drafting a concluding paragraph (ready for revision towards the end) before writing anything else, can all be good ways of easing yourself in to writing. Writer's block is rare and, it is worth repeating, typically temporary. Be patient with yourself but keep active.

# ❧ 12 ❧

# RHETORICAL QUESTIONS: SHOULD I USE THEM?

We have been a little mischievous in the title of this chapter, for its second part is itself a rhetorical question. A rhetorical question is a sentence in the form of a question, but, whether spoken or written, no answer is expected from the audience. Instead, the reply is either regarded as self-evident or posing the question is a preliminary to the author's providing the answer. It is used for effect of one sort or another, ranging from persuasion, getting the reader to pay attention, pointing out irony, or perhaps just to be amusing. It might also be used to provide a pause for readers to reflect or to take them in a related but different direction. Thus its very position in the text can also convey some information. In our case the question in the heading tells you that the section to follow will provide the answer.

If you are considering using rhetorical questions you should think about the purpose to which you want to put them. For instance, you might want to pause the flow of the text in order to summarise or maybe to pick out some especially important implication that could otherwise have been missed. In other words, a rhetorical question can be used to signpost an important point in the argument. In the following extract, a student adds a rhetorical question to the end of a paragraph that appears in the middle of her essay. The essay question asks whether 1970s feminists were right to see women as being oppressed by marriage and child-rearing. Up to this point the student has been concerned with arguing that medical technologies, such as the pill and other forms of contraception, have given women more control over childbearing. She uses her rhetorical question in order to summarise the argument thus far and then to point towards a possible new direction.

> It would certainly appear on the surface that women have enjoyed the benefits of being able to delay becoming mothers, through the use of medical technology. But has this medical technology created

the illusion of freedom that encourages women to think they can have it all – motherhood and career – only postponing their inevitable oppression? [Quotation from a second-year student's essay for a course on feminism]

Placing the rhetorical question at the end of a paragraph, towards the middle of the essay, and at the conclusion of a particular part of the argument gives the reader 'advance warning' that the next part of the essay will explore this question. The student does go on to explore how motherhood and paid work have changed over time, but she does not explicitly answer the question that she poses in the quotation above. This means that, to this extent, the use of the rhetorical question has not been completely successful. If the student had gone on to make an argument that explicitly tackles her rhetorical question and referred back to it, it would have worked much better. For instance, she could have presented her argument and then concluded by stating: 'As to the question of whether the freedom is an illusion, the answer is yes, medical technologies have indeed merely postponed the oppression of child rearing for most women.'

In this way rhetorical questions can be used as components of the very structure of your argument and help you convey the main points. Do not forget, however, that rhetorical questions are not the only way of achieving these purposes. If you are going to use rhetorical questions, it is important to use them sparingly and to ensure that you continue to use a good range of other techniques in presenting your argument.

Certainly you might also use a rhetorical question in order to have a specific effect on the reader. But, care is needed, for writers cannot be sure of controlling the reaction of their readers. Someone who did not spot the obvious answer might be left puzzled or, worse, feeling foolish. In part it may depend on the relationship you and fellow students have with your tutor. On the one hand, there may be a long-running joke among the class to which your rhetorical question could refer, but on the other, your working relationships may be more formal and business-like. So considering your audience is especially important here. If in doubt, it is better to avoid rhetorical questions of any sort as their effects can be unpredictable.

# ⇢ 13 ⇠

# HOW TO CUT YOUR ESSAY
# DOWN TO LENGTH

Tutors invariably specify how long undergraduate essays and dissertations are to be, either as numbers of words or pages. Writing to the
length required is essential, whether you are preparing an essay or a
dissertation. Learning how to do this is one of the transferable skills that
will be invaluable after graduation.

It is almost always easier to reduce a piece of writing that is too long
than to expand one that is not long enough. Too short an essay tends to
result when you have not spent enough time in the early stages of your
work reflecting on the essay title and when you have neglected to read
sufficiently widely at the beginning. If you find that you often struggle
to write at sufficient length then try to read more materials and make
more notes on these. You should also ask your tutors whether you are
providing enough explanation and exemplification of the points that
you have made in your arguments. Writing essays that are too short is
comparatively rare. It is much more common for students to find themselves having written an overlong essay or dissertation.

The ideal is to write to the length specified rather than trying to
cut down afterwards. One way to try to do this is to plan the outline
of your essay in sufficient detail, roughly allocating the length for each
section before starting to write. However, sticking to the planned allow-
ance does not always work. At times, the points you want to make end
up being more complex and take longer to set out than you expected.
Alternatively, it can feel as if new and important points present themselves as the writing proceeds and the section grows accordingly. Trying
to keep a balance between not impeding the flow of writing and repeatedly interrupting it to check the length takes practice. Getting carried
away when writing is a common cause of ending up with an essay that is
too long. This might well be a sign of your enthusiasm for the topic, but
it can also indicate that you are unsure of what you are trying to argue.

If that happens regularly, getting into the habit of checking the word length after, say, every five or six paragraphs can help you to develop a sense of length while writing.

When you have written too much, pruning your essay to reduce its length may often result in a considerably improved piece of work. A sensible start is to look for repetition. When writing an early draft you may have been so engrossed that you did not notice you said something twice, albeit using different words. Other examples of repetition result from having points in an illogical order, forcing your discussion needlessly to double-back on itself to go over things twice. The solutions are simple: cut redundant phrases and/or reorder sentences, paragraphs or even whole sections to make everything clearer and flow more smoothly.

Another tactic that is useful when cutting your essay to length is to look for passages, paragraphs, or even just a handful of sentences, which wander away from the main topic, and then simply cut out anything that has veered off at a tangent. As part of the same exercise, consider whether every point you have included is strictly relevant to answering the essay question. Teach yourself to be a bit ruthless, even if it means removing passages on topics which you think are interesting, are well written, or include a turn of phrase of which you are particularly proud. You can console yourself by creating a separate document in which to preserve them for use another time. It is much better that you have a concise, focused and well-organised essay that presents your argument clearly than that you show your tutor everything you have read, thought or written. Alternatively, if you are convinced that the point is relevant but requires too many words to make it adequately, you can summarise it extremely concisely and note its relevance, but add that it falls beyond the scope of the present essay. Adopting this strategy needs care, for you need to be sure that this point is less important than any of the other paragraphs or points that you retain in the final essay, but also that it really does need to be said. Lots of tangents and suggestions of issues outside the scope of the essay will just end up confusing the reader and give the impression that you have not thought everything through sufficiently carefully. If in doubt, it is generally better to remove material if you cannot find a good reason to include it.

# ✢ 14 ✢

# MAKING USE OF FEEDBACK

Students commonly find that some of their essays receive good scores and positive feedback whereas others are less successful. If you find that you have varying success in your assignments then learning how to make good use of feedback is particularly worthwhile. However, it is always useful for all students to reflect on how their work is received.

There are two kinds of assessment that you will encounter, each of which provides you with feedback in order to help you both develop your understanding of sociological topics and improve your skills. First, there is formative assessment, which means that your work will be graded and you will be given comments as part of the feedback. The score awarded, however, will not count towards your overall mark for the course. Second, there is summative assessment, for which you will be given a grade that does count towards your final score for the course and possibly for your degree overall.

Feedback from your formative assessments is designed to help you improve and do the best you can in your summative assessments. A summative assessment will also provide you with feedback. But this type of assignment tends to be towards the end of a course and so the feedback is to help you develop in your degree work more generally. Whether the feedback you receive is part of a formative or summative assessment, you should make sure not only to read it as a way of understanding your grade but also to make use of it to improve for your next assignment. Since the focus of our book is on the craft of writing we will concentrate our advice on how to make use of feedback in order specifically to improve your own writing.

Your tutors should provide you with useful feedback that not only explains why you got the score you did but also includes comments indicating how you could improve your work. If they do not provide you with this kind of feedback then it can be very helpful to book an appointment with them to talk through your essay and get some advice on how you could have done better. Feedback that is designed to help you improve should make some reference to what you did not do well, but also to what you did do well.

As to comments that highlight those things with which you struggled, it is vital that you take as many practical steps as you possibly can in order to improve your next assignment. It is a good idea to set aside twenty minutes or so right away, while the essay on which you received comments and the feedback itself are all fresh in your mind. Have this book alongside so you can quickly check back for another look at relevant sections. The next step is to list all the main comments you received. Then organise them according to themes: for example, grouping all the comments that relate to particular aspects of the writing process. You could then return to your essay and systematically work through it to find those parts that relate to the comments provided. It might be, for instance, that your tutor has observed that you need to improve your argument. In order to make use of this feedback, identify which parts of this book and other resources you will need to revisit and then read through them again.

Most significantly – and this is a counsel of perfection – you should then use what you have re-read to work on drafting revisions to the essay (or the particular parts of your essay) on which you have been assessed. Finally, once again book an appointment with your tutor, first sending them the revised piece, perhaps highlighting the changes that you have made. Use the appointment to discuss with your tutor how successful these changes are in addressing the issues that were raised on the earlier version of your work. Only by going back to your previous work and developing it in light of the feedback provided will you be able to speed up through improving your skills. Failing to do so risks you making the same mistakes again in your next piece of writing – which slows you down.

Students often focus on what they have not done well when looking at their feedback but it is just as important to make use of feedback that identifies what you have done well in your essays. This is because it is vital to acknowledge your success, but also because it can be difficult to know how to replicate what you did well in your next piece. For example, if you have received comments emphasising how well you have constructed your argument, you might not be completely sure what it is in this essay that you had done to which your tutor is referring. As with our advice above, it is good to collect together the comments from your feedback with the relevant portions of your essay before going back through this book to read over the appropriate sections, identifying in your own work the techniques that we have described. In this way you can more consciously and explicitly reflect on how you have successfully made use of particular techniques and be even better equipped to do so in future. Making use of feedback both on what you have done well and what you have done less well is one very good step towards producing work of more consistent quality.

# ❧ Part III ❧

# SPELLING, GRAMMAR AND PUNCTUATION

## PART III CONTENTS

# ✤ 15 ✤

# THE BASICS OF SPELLING, GRAMMAR AND PUNCTUATION

We begin the third part of the book with quotations from two novels by E. L. Doctorow, an American widely admired for his historical fiction who wrote mostly in the second half of the twentieth century. Both quotations consist of a single paragraph, the first from *Ragtime*, published in 1974:

> After the victory at Torreón, Younger Brother wore the cartridge belts crisscrossed over his chest. He was a *villista* but dreamed of going on and finding Zapata. The army rode on the tops of railroad freight cars. With the troops went their families. They lived on the tops of the trains with guns and bedding and baskets with their food. There were camp followers and babies at the breast. They rode through the desert with the cinders and smoke of the engine coming back to sting their eyes and burn their throats. They put up umbrellas against the sun. (Doctorow, 1997: 304).

The second, also just one paragraph, comes from *Loon Lake*, which came out five years later, in 1979:

> But nothing has happened, the schedule is unaltered, the drinks at certain hours, the meals at certain hours, the morning a certain time in a certain place, the afternoon and evenings all timed, the past between them unacknowledged, the past ignored, personal reactions forsworn, you-naughty-girl forborne, every breath in its good time and Bennett keeps his distance with the utmost courtesy and only sees her at the times planned for seeing, at table, or on the tennis court for her lesson or riding on the trail and she is left alone at her wish and settled

into the timed ordered planned encounters of the rich in their family life who dole out time in carefully measured amounts to each other, they even sleep in separate rooms so as not to wear out their lives on each other, so as to avoid anything like the fluid mess of most people's lives, and those who are closest to each other are as timed to be apart as anyone else. So at last she understands what wealth is, the desire for isolation and that's why never in her life before, her days and nights of time, has she enlarged this way, has her mind enlarged to the space this way, and has this voice been heard this way in reflection of herself. And the point is that she is growing to the environment, beginning to match it, and it is all beginning to make proportional sense, the timed encounters, the ceremony of courteous meetings, the space between people sharing space, the great distance to be travelled even in an obvious situation like this, so crudely obvious as to outcome the aloneness of the two of them now, not the ironic wife not the fat poet sharing the fifty thousand acres, even now the isolated distance will have to be travelled before he can allow himself to put his hands on her. And that makes her smile. Because now she will know when that time is too, it will match her awareness and nothing will shock her or surprise her because the distance he must travel is the function of his wealth, as separative as it is powerful, and she waits in grim amusement knowing that by the time something happens he will have become recognizable to her, her familiar, and their intimacy will be all that's possible for her, so natural she will wonder what it ever was that enraged her when her gangster left her sleeping and took the private train. (Doctorow, 1980: 246)

The paragraph from *Ragtime* consists of eight sentences. Though far longer, the second paragraph, from *Loon Lake*, consists of only five.

A novel is self-evidently a different genre of writing with very different purposes from those of academic work. But quoting these two paragraphs by the same author, one so much longer than the other, is to provide a speedy way of pointing out the effects on a reader that extremely long or particularly short sentences can have by way of helping you switch to thinking about writing from a grammatical point of view. Look back at the quotations to see how mood is conjured and how the character's train of thought in the second is helped by sentences so long that anyone reading it aloud has to make good use of the commas to take a breath. Contrast that with the way the first extract paints a vivid, realistic picture of movement, noise, smells and heat (among many other things), helped by short, punchy sentences. Keep these contrasting quotations in mind as you continue reading about grammar and punctuation in this third part of the book.

## THE PURPOSE OF PART III

We have written this part primarily to give you a place to turn for a quick reminder when you are in the middle of writing an essay or if you meet specific problems with spelling, grammar or punctuation. This is not designed to be your first introduction to grammar, for we assume you have already had formal English grammar lessons at school or when you first learned the language, or have picked up a working knowledge of grammar along the way. In providing a guide to what you already know, Part III covers fairly basic details of grammar and is not intended to be comprehensive (for additional reading see the Appendix).

Selected for coverage here are matters of grammar, spelling and vocabulary that we have found our students need help with most frequently and with which they repeatedly have difficulty when writing sociology essays and dissertations. Academics, writers and other professionals are not immune to such problems either. Most of us have come across minor pitfalls, such as the following, which illustrate problems with antecedents, word order and punctuation:[1]

**Advertisement from a local newspaper:**

'Pest control: wasps, flees, flies, ants, rats, bed bugs, mice, discount for OAPs.'

**Extract from a radio news report:**

'Less than 1 per cent of parents with an obese or overweight child fail to recognise it.'

**Headline in a national newspaper:**

'Heart failure patients with depression are five times more likely to die and require counselling'

---

[1] These examples were played for laughs on BBC Radio 4's *The News Quiz*, respectively: series 87, episode 2, Friday 12 June 2015; series 87, episode 2, Friday 22 May 2015; series 87, episode 2, Friday 30 May 2015.

As instances of news reporting or advertising, all three reflect problems encountered when the prevailing need is to keep to very tight word limits. But such mistakes do not only result from the shortage of space. They commonly arise when sentences are too long and poorly constructed or where there is insufficient attention to the way sentences are linked together – problems typical of the stage of writing to sort out thoughts. If you are already secure with an understanding of basic grammar when you return to edit early drafts you are much more likely to pick up and correct such mistakes.

Similarly, a grasp of the rules of English spelling as well as knowing its irregularities makes editing and proof-reading far more effective. Overlooking spelling mistakes can result, as Cutts tartly observes, in 'uninformed not uniformed police, marital not martial arts, infernal not internal disputes and pubic not public affairs' (Cutts, 2009: 226). Learning to spell helps children learn to read more fluently, and good spelling helps adults read with greater understanding and less unnecessary effort. In any case, many people – tutors included – rightly or wrongly, regard poor spelling as an indicator of poor or careless work.[2] Even more people find it completely unacceptable for students' essays to include any of the nifty ways of evading conventional spelling that developed when the length of texts (SMS) was restricted and are perpetuated in the strict limits on the number of characters of social media such as Twitter. So be sure never to write 'u' for you, 'tx' for thanks or 'gr8' for great. Just the same rationale applies to knowing how to punctuate properly. Editing and proof-reading proceed more smoothly (and even early drafting to sort out your thoughts can work more easily) if the basics of punctuation feel like second nature.

So, given that you will obviously want to avoid misleading your readers or needlessly giving them an unfavourable impression of you and your work, there are good reasons for investing some time and a little effort in refreshing your grasp of grammar, spelling and punctuation to ensure you avoid making basic mistakes. In the end you will work far more quickly as well as effectively.

## THE BASICS OF GRAMMAR

Grammar refers to the complete structure and system of language (or a particular language) and to the set of rules about how words are

---

[2] Apart from those identified as dyslexic, for whom spelling can be an unresolvable difficulty.

combined with one another. Those making an academic study of it are liable to focus on describing and reporting how a language is actually used. Here we are undeniably more prescriptive, maintaining that there is good and bad grammar, approving of some usages and disapproving of others – always using clarity as the touchstone for arriving at our judgement.[3] Not only are there fashions in whether grammar should be taught formally, what should be taught also changes, so that different generations who have learned about grammar tend to use different terminology, or even differently stated rules.

In this section we run through the basics of grammar. Obeying the rules implied is, we think, essential for writing a clear essay. The section starts by talking about sentences to help you identify what is needed to be sure of using complete sentences and then deals with some components of them. The following section sorts through the various word classes (or what in older grammatical terminology were called parts of speech) such as nouns, adjectives, conjunctions and adverbs – even though some of these will already have been mentioned beforehand. It is not vital that you learn these names – unless you are going to discuss grammar or are, perhaps, writing with someone else. It is very important, though, for you to be able to recognise the types of words to which they refer and how to use such words to write grammatically constructed, and thus clear, sentences. The section also covers verbs in more detail – especially the difference between the two types of verbs, transitive and intransitive, and the two voices, active and passive.

## Sentences

As we noted when discussing writing paragraphs, sentences represent the basic building blocks of prose writing. Sentences are simply strings of words that obey a set of rules resulting in their making sense without

---

[3] For anyone continuing to graduate study there are additional considerations. Academic writing circulates among a particular international community of users of English. This community includes those for whom English may be their second or third language. More than that, academic literature ought to have a long life, enduring over decades. Retaining standardised rules of grammar helps sustain stability and accessibility. Street slang and colloquialisms can go out of fashion pretty quickly and rapidly sound odd and out of date. Worse, their meaning may also change or be forgotten, thereby reducing accessibility and clarity.

needing anything else to be added. In other words, the string can stand alone. Sentences can typically be used for four purposes:

1. Making statements (declarative); e.g. *Your essay is very good.*
2. Asking a question (interrogative); e.g. *Is that the correct reference?*
3. Making a request, providing instructions or giving an order (imperative); *Please do not use contractions such as don't.*
4. Exclaiming (exclamative); e.g. *You always use such long words!*

Not only are statements the most common in general, they are especially likely to be so in academic writing, which has, by its nature, little scope for exclamation, commands or questions. You have probably already noticed, incidentally, that while much of this book's subject matter could be presented as a large batch of requests or even as a long list of commands, we have chosen to avoid constructing the relevant sentences as either, in an attempt to avoid sounding authoritarian or like very old-fashioned schoolteachers.

There are various forms of sentence: they are divided first into simple and multiple, which in turn is further divided into compound and complex. This section discusses all four forms, and in the process introduces clauses, which are components of sentences, and conjunctions, which are joining words.

The sentence below can be analysed grammatically (i.e. parsed) to illustrate typical components. Working through this example should reintroduce you to features you may not have thought about for several years.

The student read a textbook while his friends listened to the ball-by-ball cricket commentary through their headphones.

It contains two clauses: *(t)he student read a textbook* and *while his friends listened to the ball-by-ball cricket commentary through their headphones.* The first clause comprises three phrases: *the student, read* and *a textbook.*[4] So the two clauses of the sentence could each form a single sentence that would make sense by themselves: *(t)he student read a textbook* and *(h)is friends listened to the ball-by-ball cricket commentary through their headphones.*

---

[4] For completeness' sake, note that parsing can continue to show that the first phrase consists of two words, the second of which is, in turn, composed of two morphemes 'stu' and 'dent'.

A sentence has to consist of at least one clause; if it has just one it is known as a simple sentence (one containing two or more clauses is described as multiple,[5] a type to which we return later). Being able to identify the elements and typical patterns of a clause is particularly useful when you need to write clear but more complicated sentences than *(t)he student read a textbook*, although a simple sentence, with just one clause, is easier to start with. This simple sentence has three of five possible components, which are: subject, verb, object, complement and adverbial. Combinations of these can be used in various patterns, although a minimum for any clause is subject + verb, which is the simplest possible sentence. The subject is what or whom it is about and the verb records what the subject is, has been or will be doing. Two examples are: *(t)he student was reading* and *(t)he extraordinarily tall, red-haired student was reading*. In the first, the subject is *the student* and in the second the subject is *the extraordinarily tall, red-haired student*. In both the verb is *was reading*. The is detail – the student's height and hair colour – is still part of the subject since it is about her and not about anything else in the sentence.

Sentences can, of course, be longer. A particularly common pattern is subject + verb + object. Consider this example:

The student read a textbook.

The subject (the thing or person it is about) is *the student*, the verb (what the subject is doing) is *read* and the object (the object, person, place or thing that is not the subject) is *textbook*. Now you should be able to identify the subject, verb and object in the following three examples (check the footnote alongside each one afterwards):

'Papa's got a brand new bag.' (James Brown)[6]

'Porcupine kills large python.' (Headline, *The Telegraph*, 25 June 2015)[7]

'French President François Hollande summoned the US ambassador yesterday.' (Headline, *The Morning Star*, 25 June 2015)[8]

---

[5] Multiple sentences can be either compound or complex – see below.
[6] The subject is *Papa*, the verb is *got* and the object is *a brand new bag*.
[7] The subject is *Porcupine*, the verb is *kills* and the object is *large python*.
[8] The subject is *French President François Hollande*, the verb is *summoned* and the object is *the US ambassador*.

In all these, the object follows the verb, which is important for accurately conveying the meaning. While most people are likely to think it is self-evident that the bag has not got Papa, many (especially anyone unfamiliar with the typical behaviour of porcupines and pythons) might think it just as plausible for a large python to kill a porcupine, no matter how big it was. And it is obviously essential for the newspaper headline to report that President Hollande was doing the summoning, not the other way round.

In these three examples, more than grammar is involved in ensuring the right meaning is conveyed. Most three-year-olds perfectly well accept 'the cat sat on the mat', but would very scornfully protest that it was impossible should someone try, in all seriousness, to persuade them that 'the mat sat on the cat'. Both are correctly constructed sentences, grammatically speaking, but there is a mistake in the arrangement of items in the second version. This illustrates the difference between grammar and syntax.[9] Grammar has to do with the way sentences are formed, the rules requiring that they contain, for instance, a subject and a verb. Syntax concerns the rules that govern the order in which words are to appear.

A sentence must contain at least one main clause which, in turn, has to include a main verb.[10] A main verb is one which has a meaning on its own, one that can be found in a dictionary. Although the extract below contains two (italicised) strings of words punctuated as if they are sentences, both lack a main verb. The whole quotation appears in a novel as part of conversation, where the author is seeking to reproduce the way people speak.

> Money's tight. If one member of the family goes bust the burden falls on the rest. *All shut up together. Nothing coming in.* Silly woman chucking the stuff away. (Allingham, 2007: 95–96)

The first of the two italicised strings has no verb at all. But in spoken English, the meaning is understood as *All are shut up together*, in other words, with the silent addition of the present tense, third person plural of the verb *to be*. The second of the two italicised strings does contain a form of the verb *to come* – 'coming' is the present participle – but that is insufficient. Without the word *is* – which in speech is often omitted, and

---

[9] Simplified for present purposes: English language scholars regard the differences as more nuanced and complex.

[10] Technically, it is possible to create grammatically well-constructed sentences which consist of a single word. An example would be an imperative sentence, in which a single word command is issued: for example, 'march'.

here is implied – *coming* does not add up to a main verb. Writing it as *Nothing is coming in* immediately converts it to a full sentence complete with its main verb.

Once you understand that a simple sentence consists of a single clause, it is easy to realise that sentences can readily be extended with additional clauses. These multiple sentences divide into two types, compound and complex, and require a means of linking the clauses. The links are conjunctions. There are two types of conjunction – coordinating and subordinating – which are used in compound and complex sentences respectively (see section 'Word classes (parts of speech)' below). So a compound sentence consists of two, or more, main clauses linked by a coordinating conjunction. Here is an example from a student's essay in which the coordinating conjunction linking the clauses is in italics:

> Simon Winlow's recent work (2001) is an in-depth study of recent movements of masculine traditions in nightclub and security staff *and* will provide strong theoretical and empirical foundations for a work looking to judge the impact of historical trends in the formation of identity in an overtly masculine occupation.

Everything before the conjunction 'and' is a main clause, as is everything that follows it. A main clause is readily identified: if taken out of the multiple sentence in which it appears, it makes a sentence that can stand alone. If a clause cannot stand alone making a simple sentence, it is a different type of clause (or even a phrase). Consider this example:

> 'Nature' is a very old and complex word with diverse meanings, but in sociology it has often been seen as the opposite of culture or society. (Giddens and Sutton, 2014: 49)

Splitting this quotation readily shows that each clause makes a pair of simple sentences, each of which can stand alone:

> *'Nature' is a very old and complex word with diverse meanings.*

and

> *(I)n sociology it has often been seen as the opposite of culture or society.*

Try doing the same with another quotation from the same source (Giddens and Sutton, 2014: 79):

> The global division of labour may have many advantages for the consumer in the West, but it is also the source of much misery and exploitation.

Once again, it consists of a pair of main clauses, each of which can be converted into a sentence that can stand alone. In both instances, there is a coordinating conjunction – here it is *but*. Complex sentences also consist of one or more clauses, but in this instance there is one main clause with one or more subordinate clauses with the latter linked by subordinating conjunctions. Greater intricacy can be introduced, not least because the subordinate clauses can do the work of individual elements of a sentence, able to act as subject, object, complement (a component which completes an earlier part of the sentence) or adverbial (which adds information about a place, time, manner or the way something is done) of the main clause.

> These products have their origins in the late 19th century, when the forces of leisure and tourism market expansion, assisted in the UK by Queen Victoria's patronage of seaside and rural resorts, stimulated a demand for speciality food items associated with these places. (Tregear, 2003: 100)

*These products have their origins in the late 19th century* is the main clause, with the remainder the subordinate clause, in this case serving as an adverbial. The way of recognising the latter is to see whether it can be replaced by a single word or very short phrase without having to make a change to the grammar of the main clause. In this instance, the whole of the remainder of the sentence can be replaced by 'when demand for them went up'.

What is important in reflecting on the discussion in this section is less whether you can parse complex sentences, more that you ensure all your sentences have a main clause and, thereby, contain a main verb. And it is equally important to remember that writing complex sentences does not in itself impress anyone and thus does not automatically mean better marks. Clarity is too often the casualty of long complex sentences, with monotony just as frequently the result of long compound sentences strung together with 'and'. Shorter rather than longer sentences tend to improve clarity and make for smoother reading. Writing unduly long sentences typically happens at the stage of writing to work out your thoughts; in other words, in the very first draft. Having completed your first draft, keep a sharp eye out for very long sentences, whether compound or complex, and always consider splitting them into two (or even more!). Reflect on the difference between the very long sentences E. L. Doctorow wrote in his paragraph in *Loon Lake* and the short, staccato sentences of his *Ragtime* and think of the types of effect each has on a reader.

## Word classes (parts of speech)

This section is extremely basic, which also means it is very important, even though much of it is likely to be very familiar. It runs through what those teaching grammar used to call parts of speech, but nowadays usually call word classes. But before even getting on to word classes, a few things need to be said about words first.

Distinctions are drawn between different levels in texts; there are half-a-dozen, running from text down to sentence, clause, phrase, word and morpheme (the smallest element of language that can convey a meaning[11]). A sentence can be understood as the largest unit of grammar, at the top of a hierarchy, with each nested in the one above it. So, a sentence consists of one or more clauses, a clause consists of one or more phrases, a phrase consists of one or more words and lastly, a word consists of one or more morphemes.

Knowing about simple differences and similarities between words is useful for any writer. There is the distinction between words with similar meanings – synonyms – and those with opposite or contrasting meanings – antonyms. A thesaurus,[12] as provided in most word-processing software, lists words with a similar meaning to the word highlighted in a text, primarily providing synonyms, but often also offering one antonym. Writers find these especially useful when they need to refer to

---

[11] Some simple words are also morphemes, for instance, *sled*, *child*, *run*. Other words consist of two or more morphemes: child+ren, child+ish, run+ning, run+s, where the morphemes *ren*, *ish*, for example, convey some meaning even though they are not a word on their own.

[12] Based, it is assumed, on that first published in 1852, originally created by Peter Roget, an English lexicographer.

something more than once, without repeating the exact word in a sentence, adjacent sentences or even in a paragraph.

Then there are the distinctions between the way words sound, the way they are spelled and what they mean. Homonyms are words that are spelled and pronounced in the same way but have different meanings, for example in these four meanings of 'fair': 'fair-haired', 'fair weather', a 'fair deal' and 'the dodgem cars at the fair'. Others, homographs, are spelled the same way but pronounced differently, as well as meaning something else: 'lead', 'bow', 'perfect'. Homophones sound the same but are written differently and have quite different meanings: 'right, rite, write', 'meet, meat' and 'aloud and allowed'. It is particularly important for writers to know about homophones, not least to be sure their grammar is correct. One of the commonest mistakes with homophones concerns the three words 'there', 'their' and 'they're'. Writing 'their were three books published that year' instead of 'there were three books published that year' is a frequently observed error. Such a tiny slip does not mean readers fail to spot what has happened or that they misunderstand the intended meaning. But some readers, including tutors and examiners, regard such small mistakes as more than mere slips, treating them as indicating sloppy thinking or more general carelessness.

Thinking about word classes moves the discussion away from reflecting on aspects of words' meanings to consider the way they are used grammatically. The way words are used is the basis for grouping them into classes. There are eight word classes: nouns, verbs, adjectives, adverbs, pronouns, prepositions, conjunctions and determiners. The first four are known as open classes because the total continues to grow as new words are coined. The *Oxford English Dictionary* publishes revisions four times a year, and lists new words entering the dictionary for the first time. Instances added in 2015 are *locavore* and *the bank of mum and dad*. The other four (pronouns, prepositions, conjunctions and determiners) are closed classes to which there are no new additions. Words can move between classes, especially nouns and verbs. For example, the noun 'impact' is now very widely also used as a verb, a use that is particularly common in sociology.

Nouns and verbs are readily grasped and are the ones most people remember the most easily. Nouns are words used to refer to things, people and places as well as ideas. They can be used in the singular and the plural: 'child' and 'many children', 'method' and 'several different methods', 'household' and 'all the households in that area'. And they can be described (the technical term) by an adjective that adds some feature or quality attributable to the noun in question, often, but not always, by placing it beforehand: 'young child', 'large households' and 'quantitative method'. Types of noun can be grouped; the two most relevant for writing essays are, perhaps, proper nouns and common nouns. The first refers to unique things, places or people, and are spelled with an initial capital[13] (as well as sometimes consisting of more than one word): for example, Manchester, Marx, the Conservative Party. All the others are, as their name implies, common nouns, i.e. widespread, commonly found.

Verbs are often simply called 'doing' words – especially when teaching novices. Verbs are used to describe an action, a state, an experience or a condition, or something that happens, an occurrence. They are divided into two types, main and auxiliary. Main verbs are those that are essential to the creation of a sentence that can stand alone, such as '[M]arriage perpetuated gender inequality for several centuries' (an example from a student essay). Here the main verb is *perpetuated*, which is the third person past tense form of the verb 'to perpetuate'. The sentence '[A] different image is created in the UK, where partners aid women's prospects of employment' appears later in the same essay, illustrating the use of an auxiliary verb. In this instance, the main verb *is created* is a version of the third person present tense (in the passive voice). It is formed with the use of *is*, which here is the auxiliary verb that happens to be the present tense of the verb 'to be'. Other main auxiliaries are 'have' and 'do' (sometimes referred to as the primary auxiliaries), along with more such as 'will', 'shall', 'may', 'can', 'ought' and 'should'. Knowing about main verbs is very important for writers to help ensure that all sentences are grammatically correct. A sentence has to contain a verb.

Nouns and verbs are, obviously, linked in all kinds of ways. A simple grammatical link between them is that a plural noun takes the plural form of the verb (vice versa for the singular). Do not forget, especially when you have reached the proof-reading stage, to double-check that

---

[13] Also referred to as 'upper case'. This derives from the origins in Europe of printing and moveable type made of little pieces of metal. Each individual letter, the type, was made in the two forms, small and capitals. Each set was stored in two separate cases or boxes, one typically located above the other where the typesetter worked conveniently within reach, hence upper and lower case.

nouns and verbs agree. The student who wrote 'There's also Marxist feminists ...' is bound to know this was a slip, but did not spot it when doing the final check of the essay.

The other two word classes listed above, adjectives and adverbs, are also readily recollected, each paired with nouns and verbs respectively. Adjectives have already been mentioned. Most commonly, adjectives immediately precede the noun they describe – the 'large' household, the 'smaller' child, the 'easiest' method. Those examples also illustrate the way adjectives can have different forms to signal a rank or grade; 'large' has the comparative form 'larger' and the superlative form 'largest'. Adverbs modify or qualify verbs. The words 'modify' or 'qualify' are, once again, the technical terms, though adverbs have the same sort of relation to verbs as adjectives do to nouns in that they both say something more about them. The italicised words in the following sentence illustrate first an adverb modifying (or qualifying) the verb 'lived', and then an adjective describing the noun 'household'.

They lived *happily* in the *larger* household.

The remaining four – pronouns, prepositions, conjunctions and determiners – are the closed word classes. Pronouns stand in for nouns (noun phrases or even other pronouns). Their use can help reduce repetition, which many writers want to do, simply because reading the same word repeatedly can become extremely tedious. Paying a little attention to the various pronouns is valuable, since sorting out common mistakes relies on being able to identify them. Pronouns are divided into different groups: personal (her, it, I, you, etc.); possessive (mine, hers, its, theirs, etc.); reflexive (myself, yourselves, oneself, etc.); demonstrative (this, those, that, etc.); interrogative (whose, what, which, who, etc.); relative (whom, which, that, etc.); and indefinite (someone, nobody, everything, all, etc.). And there is a good reason for giving some thought to one of these groups in particular, the possessive. Refreshing your memory of the pronouns in this group will help protect you from one of the commonest examples of the misplaced apostrophe. The possessive pronouns are: mine, ours, yours, hers, his, its, theirs. The trick is to remind yourself of the list and remember that, apart from 'mine', they all end in 's'. Doing this will help you avoid confusing the spelling of 'its' (which is the possessive pronoun) with 'it's' (which is the contraction of 'it is').

Prepositions are words which govern (again the technical term) and mostly precede nouns and pronouns (or noun phrases, phrases which do the work of a noun). They primarily provide information about direction, time or location, thus expressing a relation to another word or part of the sentence. The list of prepositions is long, including 'above', 'beyond', 'down', 'until', 'to', 'by', 'towards', 'over', 'behind', 'here', 'except', 'past', 'since'. There are also two-, three- and even four-word prepositions: because of, on top of, in the face of.

Conjunctions and determiners are the final two word classes. Conjunctions have already been introduced when discussing multiple sentences above. They are divided into two: coordinating conjunctions such as 'or', 'and', 'but' and subordinate conjunctions such as 'because', 'although', 'when', 'if'. Their serving as links between main clauses has already been discussed. They may also join words and phrases. Adopting a simple characterisation, determiners are words or phrases which in some way limit meaning. Examples are 'a', 'this', 'the', 'every', 'many', 'some'.

## Clauses and phrases

Both clauses and phrases are strings of words, just as sentences are. But as has already been noted when introducing them earlier, clauses contain verbs. If a clause contains a main verb it constitutes a sentence; put the other way round, a simple sentence consists of a single clause. A shorthand way of distinguishing phrases from clauses is that the former do not have verbs. By and large, phrases consist of more than a single word, although when examined technically in grammatical terms, a phrase may consist of just one word. The following sentence has been divided into phrases:

> The Columbia study | established clearly | that | diffusion | was | a social process. (Rogers, 2003: 65)

Compare it with:

> The | Columbia | study established | clearly that | diffusion was a | social process.

The second version is broken up into what are self-evidently unnatural divisions with words grouped together which do not function as a grammatical unit. There are five types of phrase, each named after the part of speech which is central to its structure, giving: noun, verb, adjective, adverb and preposition phrases. 'The Columbia study' is a noun phrase where the main word is the noun *study*, while 'established clearly' is a verb phrase in which the main word is the verb *established.*

## Intransitive and transitive verbs

The meanings of verbs are conveyed in various ways. Some verbs need nothing extra (technically, they need no 'complementation'). They are complete in themselves. These are intransitive verbs, for instance:

'He *laughed* all the way to the bank.'
'More people *died*.'
'Incomes have *risen* since the 1950s.'

Others need something more, commonly an object, to complete the meaning. In this case, verbs are used transitively, as in the following sentences in which the transitive verb takes a direct object:

She *wrote* the essay.
'Sociologists *define* religion as a cultural system of commonly shared beliefs and rituals.' (Giddens, 2006: 534)

The italicised verbs *wrote* and *define* are transitive, taking the direct object *essay* and *religion.*

The distinction between intransitive and transitive verbs just presented is heavily simplified. But it will serve well enough to help you to write clear sentences. If you want to learn to recognise each type of verb when you read, a shorthand way of working out a direct object is to see if it makes sense as an answer when you put the verb into a question: 'what did she write?' or 'what do sociologists define?' The important thing is to remember to include an object when using a transitive verb.

One of the marked changes in English usage of the last two decades or so is the way more verbs have been switched from intransitive to transitive use and, occasionally, vice versa. So nowadays it is possible to '*browse* the shelves', whereas once it would only have made sense in everyday speech to answer the bookseller's asking 'Can I help you?' with 'No thanks, I would just like to *browse*'. So *browse*, formerly an intransitive verb, is used transitively nowadays. The opposite can also be detected: once it would only have been possible to *commit* oneself to some course of action – the transitive verb *to commit* taking the object *oneself*, a reflexive pronoun. Nowadays, people are simply expected *to commit*.

## Active and passive voice

Voice provides information about the part played by different people or things. Voice is active or passive and changes the relationship between the subject and object of a verb. Compare the following:

> Once released into the environment, GMOs may set off a string of knock-on effects that will be difficult to monitor and control.

> A string of knock-on effects that will be difficult to monitor and control may be set off by GMOs once they are released into the environment.

The first sentence is what Giddens wrote (2006: 963), where *GMOs* are the subject, *set off* is the verb and *knock-on effects* the object. The second is the sentence rewritten in the passive voice, where this time *knock-on effects* is the subject, *set off* still the verb and *GMOs* is now the object.

It is conventional in the natural and life sciences to write up research in the passive voice. This device is held to be appropriate as part of helping to underscore that scientific work is considered to be objective, with the results obtaining no matter who undertakes the experimental work. If reference is needed to the experimenter or author of the article, it is common enough to find that the third person singular or plural is used; the researcher oversaw the experiment, the author undertook the calculations. Sociologists vary as to whether they follow that same convention, or whether they are willing to use the active voice and first person. Many argue that using the active voice is important not simply with respect to debates about the objectivity or otherwise of both the sciences and social sciences, but as a means of ensuring agency is exposed to view and thus is incorporated into the analysis. As such, you are more likely to find sociologists writing 'I conducted interviews' or 'In this analysis I present my preliminary findings'. Selecting a voice for your essays should follow the conventions that are most appropriate to your situation. Some departments prefer students to use the active voice and some the passive. Consult your tutors on this and consider discussing with them some of the reasons behind these conventions. Those reasons can be important parts of your education in methodological issues as well as in writing style.

## THE BASICS OF PUNCTUATION

Punctuation refers to the set of marks in a text designed to help readers understand, interpret and follow what they are reading. It is an integral component of the way the page looks.[14] It is not just that the beginning and end of paragraphs can be identified by indenting the first line or adding a line space between blocks of text; sentences are marked off from one another with full stops; words are separated by spaces between them and so on. The value of punctuation for conveying meaning can very readily be seen in the way it helps limit ambiguity. A neat example is the one well publicised in the UK when Lynne Truss chose *Eats, Shoots and Leaves* as the title of her book on the 'zero tolerance approach to punctuation'.[15] While she has been criticised for being a purist who is reluctant to recognise that language is not static, her remark that '(P)roper punctuation is both the sign and the cause of clear thinking' is hard to dismiss altogether (Truss, 2003: 202).

One way of thinking about punctuation is that it is the written version, represented on paper, of pauses in spoken English, of changes in the pitch of the voice and of variations in emphasis. The pitch of the voice tends to drop and the pace of speech even slows fractionally when arriving at the end of a statement.[16] This is represented by a full stop. In contrast, the pitch of the voice tends to rise towards the end of an interrogative sentence, as a way of signalling that a question is being asked. The question mark serves the same purpose on the page. Commas also convey meaning, signalling the very brief pauses that help us understand what is being said. Commas are also useful for literally and

---

[14] Other features of the layout are the size of the margins, the location of any headings (e.g. in the centre or to one side), the font, the point size and so forth.

[15] She derived the title from a joke, an explanation of which is available at http://pet-fun.blogspot.co.uk/2006/09/joke-eats-shoots-and-leaves.html (accessed 23 July 2015).

[16] Except among some younger generations, which have adopted an interrogative rise in pitch at the end of a declarative statement, reputedly originating in Australia. This makes it sound as if all sentences are questions and can be quite frustrating for other speakers unused to this way of speaking.

metaphorically taking a breath, especially in long sentences. Try reading out loud the paragraph E. L. Doctorow wrote in *Loon Lake* which is quoted at the beginning of this part of the book. All those commas help you breathe. This way of reflecting the manner in which people speak was the purpose of earlier forms of punctuation. For the last two centuries, however, punctuation has been based on grammatical structures, notably sentences and clauses, which are particularly important structures (Chalker and Weiner, 1994: 324) as well as some sorts of phrase. All these are discussed in the remainder of this section, which concentrates first on full stops and commas, and then on colons and semi-colons. While it is invaluable to get the basics of punctuation well fixed in your mind for your writing, the editing and proof-reading stages are the best time to consider whether the punctuation supports the meaning you are trying to convey or whether you have omitted a full stop or misplaced a comma and thus twisted the sense.

## Full stops and commas

Full stops and commas are among the most frequently used punctuation marks, together with capital letters, apostrophes, quotation marks, brackets, colons and semi-colons. Others, possibly less frequently used, are exclamation marks, question marks, dashes, ellipses and hyphens. Any of your essays is bound to include the first six just listed, while it is much less likely to need exclamation marks, question marks or dashes. But you could write a very good essay without once using either colons or semi-colons – except, perhaps, in the way the references are laid out or when quoting directly what someone else has written. And you may never need hyphens to indicate that a word has been broken between the end of one line and the start of the next since, typically, word-processing software settings can avoid having to break words in this way.

A full stop (known as a period in American English) is essential when punctuating a declarative[17] sentence correctly. The capital letter of the first word identifies the beginning of the sentence and the full stop after the last word indicates its end. With its subject and main verb, these complete a properly written declarative sentence. That much you are bound to know so well that it barely needed saying. Equally, you are bound to

---

[17] The type that makes a statement.

know that a full stop is also used in the initials of someone's name, for example, *C. Wright Mills* or *J. K. Rowling*, and after abbreviations such as *ed.* or *etc.*, although you may well have noticed that the latter convention is no longer used quite so strictly.

Conventions for using commas tend to give students more difficulty. It is probably more common to find students using too many than too few, as in the following examples which come from different term papers:

'In this, what is often considered, secularised and rational contemporary society …'

'… claims to be, "getting in the door" or getting access …'

Detecting the superfluous commas is easy: simply read both extracts out loud and pause at each one and you will hear that it does not make very good sense and the flow is interrupted.

To use commas with confidence requires some grasp of clauses and phrases. Recollect that clauses and phrases are strings of words contained inside sentences. Each has identifiable characteristics, as we described earlier. Clauses differ from phrases in that they have to contain a verb, while phrases can consist of a single word. A simple sentence consists of a single clause and thereby only needs punctuation for a sentence – initial capital letter, full stop at the end. 'The cat sat on the mat.' If you expand the sentence you might or might not need to add commas. For example, in this sentence there is no need for a comma: 'The tabby cat sat on the red mat.' Adjectives have been added to describe the cat and the mat. Adding an adverb would normally not introduce the need for a comma either: 'The tabby cat sat comfortably on the red mat.' All these are examples of simple sentences, punctuated in the familiar, straightforward and basic way.

A compound sentence, however, consisting of more than one clause, typically needs the use of one or more commas. For example:

The following survey is based on twenty-one examples between 1554 and 1594, and concentrates on the kitchen, cooking and food equipment rather than on furniture, silver- and display-ware, clothes or linen. (White, 2000: 123)

The first clause is 'The following survey is based on twenty-one examples between 1554 and 1594'; its end is indicated with a comma. It is then joined by the conjunction 'and' to the second clause, which in turn contains several phrases separated by commas such as 'cooking and food equipment rather than on furniture'.

While there are several technically specific uses for commas, we suggest that for present purposes, the use of commas can be thought of as relatively straightforward provided the basics are borne in mind. So, think not only of grammatical structures of clauses and phrases, but also of the way speech has pauses to convey meaning and to allow speakers to breathe. If in doubt, read the passage you are trying to punctuate out loud; this can often help tell you where commas are necessary or redundant. Keep in mind that our experience suggests that it is more common for students to use too many commas than too few.

## Colons and semi-colons

If you really wanted, you could write a good essay without using either colons or semi-colons.[18] They can, however, be useful. Their purposes are specific. Both are used within a sentence. Colons are commonly used to introduce something, a list, a sub-title, an example or a quotation, especially if either of the latter two is indented. You will find a colon is especially useful when you are about to add a quotation, for it also indicates where what you are writing ends and the words that someone else has said or written begin.[19] The following example – which of course follows the convention being illustrated as well as twice exemplifying the use of indentation to signal the use of a quotation – comes from Erving Goffman's first book, *The Presentation of Self in Everyday Life*:

> Orwell, speaking of waiters and speaking from the backstage point of view of dishwashers, provides us with an example:

---

[18] Even if you happen to be unfamiliar with the names semi-colon and colon, you will know them when used to create emoticons using a keyboard. According to Microsoft's online support for Office, a smiley face :) is created with a colon followed by a bracket, while a wink ;) is conveyed by typing a semi-colon followed by a bracket. https://support.office.com/en-us/article/Keyboard-shortcuts-for-emoticons-dda403dc-ffe9-4cbb-9b9f-aed845ff8b8c (accessed 7 February 2016).

[19] This way of visually separating text written by two different people is mirrored in the use of a colon to introduce dialogue in a novel or in a film script to separate the words that are uttered from the indication – e.g. the name – of who is saying them.

> It is an instructive sight to see a waiter going into a hotel dining-room. As he passes the door a sudden change comes over him. (1956: 74)

Leafing through this book will rapidly provide further examples of colons and indentation used with quotations.

While commas are most frequently used to separate a sentence's clauses (and phrases), a semi-colon can be used to divide a sentence in which you have two closely related things to say. In this instance, the semi-colon takes the place of a full stop between a pair of sentences. In other words, each clause could be written as a sentence on its own, but you want to emphasise their closeness by putting them together into a single, longer one divided by the semi-colon. The test of whether you should use a semi-colon or comma is to check whether both parts of the sentence either side of the punctuation mark are complete sentences and can stand alone. Here is an instance which slipped past a journal's copy-editor and which fails the test:

> Such questions redirect attention from individual 'inconsistencies' towards social and political processes; like the social distribution of responsibility for key food issues, the role of trust, and power to change conditions in the food supply chain. (Kjærnes, 2012: 146)

The passage which follows the semi-colon, 'like the social distribution of responsibility for key food issues, the role of trust, and power to change conditions in the food supply chain', is a list whose role is to illustrate the point in the clause that precedes the semi-colon. Since it contains no main verb and thus cannot stand as a sentence on its own, the use of a semi-colon is incorrect, and either a comma should have been used or a colon. If a colon is used, the items on the list could be separated with a semi-colon. This illustrates a further use of a semi-colon: to separate the items on a list, especially if they are phrases and not single words.

Here are alternative ways in which Kjærnes's sentence could be correctly punctuated, with the first example following the form already illustrated in the example about kitchen, cooking and food equipment:

> Such questions redirect attention from individual 'inconsistencies' towards social and political processes, like the social distribution of responsibility for key food issues, the role of trust, and power to change conditions in the food supply chain.

Or:

> Such questions redirect attention from individual 'inconsistencies' towards social and political processes, such as: the social distribution of responsibility for key food issues; the role of trust; and power to change conditions in the food supply chain.

Many prefer the second alternative, especially if their list is long. This is because the use of the colon which introduces the list at the end of the first part of the sentence alerts readers to the point where the list begins. The colon usefully catches their attention.

## The apostrophe

> '… new media is in it's infancy and it is hard to say …'

> 'new media has several success stories based on it's use for work'

> 'One of the most important lenses through which we must look at new medias affect on the individual is through everyday life and work.'

> 'One of the main arguments in this research is how the stereotypical representation of male victims impacts heavily on the manner in which authorities deal with cases.'

> 'One main factor in my reasoning's for choosing qualitative research in my approach to this topic was the idea that it allowed me to explore the issues however deeply I wanted to.'

The first three examples (the third of which also illustrates the misuse of 'affect' for 'effect', for which check the final section of this book) come from an essay with five superfluous apostrophes and a couple of missing ones. The fourth comes from a different essay and it requires a bit of time to realise that 'impacts' is a verb not a noun – the impacts do not belong to the victims but affect the authorities dealing with cases. And the final one is from a different student's work in a sentence that deserves to be redrafted anyway. If, like these students, you struggle to remember how to use apostrophes (or, come to that, certain spellings, or grammatical rules), make a point of being extra careful when proof-reading and look out for snags you already know are likely to trip you up.

Apostrophes are used for several purposes. One is to indicate a contraction – where a letter has been left out of a word, or usually between a pair of words. So 'cannot' can be written '*can't*', 'is not' can be written '*isn't*' and 'it is' can be written '*it's*'. This is the use of an apostrophe which we have already suggested you should avoid, since some tutors regard its informality as carelessness, being unduly casual or even slang. So try not to use can't, isn't and it's.

You will need another use of apostrophes quite often. This indicates the possessive form of nouns and pronouns. These are examples where the noun is in the singular: 'the essay's cover sheet'; 'the student's view on the matter'; 'the lecturer's notes'. The rules for a plural noun depend on whether or not it already ends in *s* and determine whether the apostrophe precedes or follows the *s* that has to be added to indicate possession. If the noun does not already end in *s*, then add '*s*, as in 'men's commitment to the cause' or 'the police's actions were criticised'. If, however, the plural noun already ends in *s*, then place the apostrophe after the *s* and use *s*': for example, 'those colleagues' decisions were misguided'.

As we showed earlier, the contraction *it's* tends to cause the greatest difficulty. This is because the same three letters make the possessive pronoun *its* (as you will remember, the other possessive pronouns are mine, ours, yours, hers, his and theirs). People tend to muddle up two separate uses of the apostrophe. Learning to distinguish the use to indicate a contraction – a missing letter – from the use to indicate a possessive will improve your accurate use of the apostrophe overnight.

## CONCLUDING REMARKS

It is always easy for someone who is sure-footed about spelling, confident about their knowledge of basic grammar and does not find themselves fretting indecisively as to where (or even whether) to put an apostrophe to treat what has been covered in this final part of the book as far too simple for undergraduates. Even those fortunate enough to be completely familiar with all that has been covered in Part III can still find they suffer sudden doubts or lapses of memory. So whether this final section is just a bit of a refresher or has set out things you were only half sure about, you will find that reminding yourself of these very basic features of sentence construction, of the distinction between colons and semi-colons and keeping the number of commas you use in check will make your writing life a lot smoother.

# COMMON SPELLING AND VOCABULARY MISTAKES

## COMMON SPELLING MISTAKES

Certain spelling mistakes are widespread. They can be found in all kinds of writing, including drafts of research reports and even Official Statistics, and are made even by experienced writers, despite the availability of spell-checkers.[1] To be fair, some spelling mistakes cannot be detected by spell-checkers. These are cases where a correctly spelled word is used, but it is the wrong word. Familiar ones are: *compliment* (meaning polite admiration) or *complimentary* (free of charge) instead of *complement* (something that completes, a full set) or *complementary* (going well with, matching). Avoiding these kinds of mistakes is difficult and involves very careful proof-reading. Remember that spelling mistakes of many kinds can be introduced during the copy-editing process, in which you are checking the sense of what you have written together with considering the order of the argument. This is another reason why it is important to treat copy-editing and proof-reading as separate processes and to give yourself time to do both well.

Common spelling mistakes are also individual. Most of us, even if we are very good at spelling, have some words which continue to trip us up. For many people, these are words that have letters in somewhat unexpected places, or in which the sound of the word does not quite match

[1] This is a formal term to identify certain government publications. In the UK ' "official statistics" [are] all those statistical outputs produced by the UK Statistics Authority's executive office (the Office for National Statistics), by central Government departments and agencies, by the devolved administrations in Northern Ireland, Scotland and Wales, and by other Crown bodies (over 200 bodies in total)'. www.statisticsauthority.gov.uk/national-statistician/types-of-official-statistics (accessed 22 July 2015).

the spelling, such as *accessible, accommodate, exercise, necessary, paralleled* and *privilege*. Many of us too have to work hard at distinguishing between *advice*, which is a noun, and *advise*, the verb, or rather more taxing, the noun *practice* and the verb *practise*,[2] which are homophones (sound the same).

To make matters worse, conventions for English spellings have developed differently in different parts of the world where the language is used. The spelling of the same word in what Microsoft calls UK English and American English differ in familiar and evident ways: for instance, respectively, *labour* and *labor*, *behaviour* and *behavior*, *travelled* and *traveled*, *programme* and *program*, although in UK English the American *program* is used in computing. UK English is the default choice for students in the UK and American English for those in the US; elsewhere, the choice is less clear. Australia and New Zealand use a combination of UK English and American English spellings, for example. Outside of the UK, unless your department or school, or, indeed, your tutors, specify which you are to use for your essays, it may not matter which you choose. Be very sure, of course, to be consistent.

We cannot list all words that are difficult to spell, but here are some of the common spelling mistakes which we come across in our students' work, and which, as we shall recommend when it comes to thinking about vocabulary, you would be well advised to learn to get right since they crop up frequently in sociological writing. For a much more extensive list of common spelling mistakes, see Gordon Jarvie's (1993) *Bloomsbury Grammar Guide* or Bill Bryson's (2002) *Dictionary of Troublesome Words.*

**Breach** means a break, gap or opening, for example 'a breach of social norms', whereas **breech** means the lower part of something, for example in 'breech birth'.

**Centre** is the spelling in UK English and **center** in American English.

**Criteria** is a plural and refers to several elements, for example 'there were criteria she did not consider', whereas **criterion** is the singular, for example 'the most important criterion is clarity'.

**Data** is a plural and refers to a collection of items, for example 'these data point towards a pattern', whereas **datum** is the singular. It is rare that you should need to refer to a singular datum and so whenever referring to data you should be careful to use a plural to describe them. Note that everyday speech and much journalism commonly uses data as if singular; the plural (correct) form continues, however, in academic writing for the moment.

---

[2] In American English both noun and verb are spelled *practice*, making it potentially harder still for the unwary.

*Discreet* means careful, for example 'she can be trusted with the information because she is very discreet', whereas *discrete* means unrelated or different, for example 'there are discrete reasons for these two voting patterns'.

*Enquiry* is the spelling in UK English most often used in an informal way, for example 'I enquired as to where the bathroom was', whereas *inquiry* is generally used to mean a more formal inquiry such as might be made by the police or a government body.

*Its* means belonging to, for example 'its wheels have fallen off', whereas *it's* means 'it is', for example 'it's raining and pouring'.

*Lead* is a verb meaning to lead someone or something, for example 'to lead a nation towards economic collapse', whereas *led* is the past tense of the same verb, for example 'he led the nation into war'. *Lead* is also a noun, meaning the metal.

*Lose* means to have mislaid something, whereas *loose* means not tightly fixed.

*Practice* in UK English is a noun, for example 'practice will improve your ability', whereas *practise* is the verb, for example 'he sent me to practise for my exams'. In American English, *practice* is always spelled with a 'c'.

*Principle* is a noun meaning a fundamental truth or law, such as in 'there are a number of Christian principles', whereas *principal* is a noun meaning the chief, the main one, head of or first, for example 'the principal of the school'.

*Stationery* is a collective noun for paper and associated items, whereas *stationary* is an adjective to describe the condition of not moving, for example 'the vehicle was stationary'.

## COMMON VOCABULARY MISTAKES

Understanding what words mean and using them as correctly as possible self-evidently helps you to write clearly. The best tip we can offer is: always make the effort to use a dictionary when you come across a word that is new to you. Do not just hope you understand or rely on guesswork. Obviously doing either risks learning the wrong meaning and/or misleading your reader when you venture to use it yourself. Using online dictionaries can help and there are three or four well-known and authoritative ones which will be listed by any search engine. Quite often dictionaries offer alternative definitions which can make learning the meaning of a new word easier. Looking a word up helps you remember it and expand your own vocabulary, giving you additional words to be used with confidence. Looking up words regularly will help you to avoid using the wrong word. And take care: using the wrong word can result from relying on the word-processing software's thesaurus, which provides synonyms that are not always appropriate to the meaning you are trying to convey.

The choice of vocabulary can, in some circumstances, carry very strong connotations of power. And, of course, selected words become 'politically incorrect', with objections raised if they are used. If using them cannot be avoided, reference may well be made euphemistically – for example, a journalist writing 'the "n" word' to evade quoting the reprehensible use of the old racial segregationist word 'nigger'. All the same, members of the Black Power movement of the 1960s deliberately used the word 'black', to reclaim it from segregationist usage and proclaim that 'black is beautiful'. Similarly, vocabulary now deemed sexist is to be avoided with the use of sex-neutral terms recommended. This means, for instance, avoiding words that are sex-specific when intending to refer to everyone or all occupying that role or position. To avoid mistakes in vocabulary of this sort, replace the sexist term with a sex-neutral one: for example, replace *policeman* with *police officer, headmaster* with *head-teacher* and so on. It also means thinking very carefully about pronouns and not using *he* or *his* when intending to refer to both women and men. There are various alternatives: use the phrase '*him or her*' or even '*him/her*' or '*s/he*'. We have adopted the less cumbersome alternative of using plural forms ('they', 'them' and 'their') whenever feasible.

Of course, languages are constantly changing as people use them. What many would consider mistakes now may well become accepted meanings in the future. All the same, tutors often notice and get irritated by what they consider incorrect usages or malapropisms. Once again this can risk their thinking of you as careless or ignorant. Some pairs of words are frequently confused. You would be well advised to study the list below. Again, for a much more extensive list of common mistakes, see Gordon Jarvie's (1993) *Grammar Guide* or Bill Bryson's (2002) *Dictionary of Troublesome Words*.

*Adverse* refers to something which is unfavourable, for example an adverse review of a book, whereas *averse* refers to the state of being disinclined to be involved with something, for example 'I am averse to giving verbal presentations'.

*Affect* is both a noun and a verb: the verb *to affect* something is to change it in some way; the noun *affect* refers to the realm of emotion, a term commonly used by psychologists and psychiatrists, and typically pronounced differently from *affect* as a verb, by placing the emphasis on the first syllable, rather than the second. *Affect* is often confused with *effect* and vice versa.

*Ambiguous* means the meaning is unclear; *ambivalent* means being undecided or in two minds about something or someone.

*Authoritative* means knowledgeable or expert, whereas *authoritarian* means dictatorial or controlling.

*Can* means that it is possible, whereas *may* means that it is allowed, for example 'you can break the law but you may not do so'.

*Centre* means the point that is equidistant from all sides and so should not be followed by the word 'around', as in 'this chapter centres around the topic', which should instead be 'this chapter centres on the topic'.

*Data* refers to the collection of raw material, for example a number of interview transcripts or a spreadsheet of figures, and is not synonymous with *information*, which refers to data which have not been interpreted, so you should say 'the data are yet to be interpreted' or 'there is growing information about the events in question'.

*Definite* means certain, whereas *definitive* means the most authoritative.

*Disinterested* does not mean *uninterested*; it means impartial or indifferent.

*Effect* is also both a noun and a verb: the verb *to effect* something is to make something happen; the noun *effect* is the result of something happening.

*Fewer* is used in relation to plural nouns, for example 'there are fewer teachers than last year', whereas *less* is used in relation to singular nouns, for example 'less forest was destroyed than in the previous decade'. So it would not be correct to say 'less teachers' just as it would not be correct to say 'fewer forest'.

*Imply* means hint at something or other, *infer* means deduce or work something out from the information provided.

*Latter* means the second or last item, for example 'of bridges and balloons only the latter can be carried by a child', whereas *former* means the first item, for example 'of bridges and balloons only the former can support the weight of a car'.

*Militate* means to have force, whereas *mitigate* means to make something less serious.

*Refute* means to demonstrate conclusively that something is wrong or incorrect, for example 'he refuted the allegation that he had miscounted the votes'. Be sure that when you use the term you mean something has been demonstrated without any doubt. Alternatively, use 'challenge', 'deny' or 'dispute'.

*Specially* means tailor-made, for example 'he made it specially for the audience', whereas *especially* means exceptionally, for example 'she was an especially gifted politician'.

# APPENDIX: FURTHER READING

In this brief selection the first four entries are especially useful for undergraduates. The next three were all written for postgraduates and beyond, but could be helpful for writing undergraduate dissertations. The final group of entries are accessible examples specifically about grammar which are likely to be in your university library or cost relatively little, with one open access source.

## FOR UNDERGRADUATE LEVEL

Black, Jeremy and MacRaild, Donald M. (2007) *Studying History*. 3rd edn. Basingstoke: Palgrave Macmillan.

Includes discussions of both theories and concepts and dissertation writing for students of history, and overlaps from that disciplinary point of view with the coverage in Part I of this book on principles and practice, which will be particularly useful for students writing theoretical dissertations and/or analysing documents.

Burns, Tom and Sinfield, Sandra (2003) *Essential Study Skills: The Complete Guide to Success at University*. London: Sage Publications.

Wide-ranging guide to being a university student covering essentials such as time management, being organised and preparing for exams as well as academic reading skills.

Cottrell, S. (2005) *Critical Thinking Skills: Developing Effective Analysis and Argument*. Basingstoke: Palgrave Macmillan.

Explores in fine detail some of the ways in which you can improve your critical apprehension of texts, by helping you to search for patterns, inconsistencies, reasoning, evidence and conclusions. Provides a lot of activities and tests for students to use in developing these skills.

Osmond, Alex (2013) *Academic Writing and Grammar for Students*. London: Sage Publications.

Covers academic writing across the humanities and social sciences. Includes much basic information and is particularly useful for first-year students.

## FOR POSTGRADUATE LEVEL

Becker, Howard S. (2007 [1986]) *Writing for Social Scientists*. 2nd edn. Chicago: University of Chicago Press.

Advanced level but very readable, based on experience of teaching graduate students. Becker was not expecting the reception of the first edition of this book to be so enthusiastic and heartfelt, but it was sufficient to prompt him to update it to take account of the ubiquity of personal computers.

Swales, John M. and Feak, Christine B. (2012) *Academic Writing for Graduate Students*. 3rd edn. Michigan: Michigan University Press.

Advanced-level discussion, including detailed coverage of writing research papers and articles.

Wallace, Michael and Wray, Alison (2016) *Critical Reading and Writing for Postgraduates*. 3rd edn. London: Sage Publications.

Advanced-level discussion, with a worked example of a critical analysis of a published article.

## GRAMMAR

Murphy, R. (2012) *English Grammar in Use*. Cambridge: Cambridge University Press.

Written specially for learners of English, with flexible availability including a fully downloadable app.

Open University (2016) *English Grammar in Context*. Free downloadable course: www.open.edu/openlearn/education/educational-technology-and-practice/educational-practice/english-grammar-context/content-section-0 (last updated 24 March 2016; accessed 3 April 2016).

This is an open access course but will require you to register as a user on the website.

Seely, John (2009) *Oxford A–Z of Grammar & Punctuation*. Oxford: Oxford University Press.

A dictionary-style text including helpful cross-referencing which is useful for quick reference.

Trask, R. L. (2000) *The Penguin Dictionary of English Grammar*. London: Penguin.

Valuable, more advanced coverage for students looking to improve their depth of understanding.

Ward, Lesley J. and Woods, Geraldine (2007) *English Grammar for Dummies®*. UK edn. Chichester: Wiley.

Familiar '*For Dummies®*' treatment supporting further study.

# REFERENCES

Allingham, Margery (2007) *More Work for the Undertaker*. London: Vintage Books (first published 1949).

Blumer, Herbert (2004) *George Herbert Mead and Human Conduct*. Edited by Thomas J. Morrione. Walnut Creek, CA: AltaMira Press.

Bryson, B. (2002) *Bryson's Dictionary of Troublesome Words: A Writer's Guide to Getting It Right*. New York: Broadway Books.

Carter, Ronald and McCarthy, Michael (2006) *Cambridge Grammar of English: A Comprehensive Guide – Spoken and Written English Grammar and Usage*. Cambridge: Cambridge University Press.

Chalker, Sylvia and Weiner, Edmund (1994) *The Oxford Dictionary of English Grammar*. Oxford: Clarendon Press.

Chapman, Myra and Mahon, Basil (1986) *Plain Figures*. London: Her Majesty's Stationery Office.

Cutts, Martin (2009) *Oxford Guide to Plain English*. Oxford: Oxford University Press.

Doctorow, E. L. (1980) *Loon Lake*. London: Macmillan (first published privately, 1979).

Doctorow, E. L. (1997) *Ragtime*. New York: Modern Library (Random House) (first published 1974).

Foucault, M. (1981) *History of Sexuality Volume 1: An Introduction*. New York: Pantheon Books.

Giddens, Anthony (1984) *The Constitution of Society*. Cambridge: Polity Press.

Giddens, Anthony (2006) *Sociology*. Cambridge: Polity Press.

Giddens, Anthony and Sutton, Philip W. (2014) *Essential Concepts in Sociology*. Cambridge: Polity Press.

Goffman, Erving (1956) *The Presentation of Self in Everyday Life*. Monograph No. 2. Edinburgh: University of Edinburgh.

Jackson, Howard (2002) *Grammar and Vocabulary: A Resource Book for Students*. London: Routledge.

Jarvie, Gordon (1993) *Bloomsbury Grammar Guide: Grammar Made Easy*. London: Bloomsbury.

Kjærnes, Unni (2012) 'Ethics and Action: A Relational Perspective on Consumer Choice in the European Politics of Food'. *Journal of Agricultural and Environmental Ethics* 25: 145–162.

Mead, G. H. (1934) *Mind, Self, and Society: From the Standpoint of a Social Behaviorist*. Chicago: Chicago University Press.

Mills, C. Wright (1959) *The Sociological Imagination*. Oxford: Oxford University Press.

Morgan, David (2009) *Acquaintances: The Space between Intimates and Strangers*. Milton Keynes: Open University Press.

Nazroo, J. (2003) 'The Structuring of Ethnic Inequalities in Health: Economic Position, Racial Discrimination and Racism'. *American Journal of Public Health* 93(2): 277–284.

Open University (2016) *English Grammar in Context*. Free downloadable course: www.open.edu/openlearn/education/educational-technology-and-practice/educational-practice/english-grammar-context/content-section-0 (last updated 24 March 2016; accessed 3 April 2016).

Partridge, E. (1963) *Usage and Abusage: A Guide to Good English*. Harmondsworth: Penguin.

Pinker, Steven (2014) *The Sense of Style: The Thinking Person's Guide to Writing in the 21st Century*. London: Allen Lane.

Rogers, Everett M. (2003) *Diffusion of Innovations*. 5th edn. New York: Free Press.

Seely, John (2009) *Oxford A–Z of Grammar & Punctuation*. Oxford: Oxford University Press.

Trask, R. L. (2000) *The Penguin Dictionary of English Grammar*. London: Penguin.

Tregear, Angela (2003) 'From Stilton to Vimto: Using Food History to Re-think Typical Products in Rural Development'. *Sociologia Ruralis* 43(2): 91–107.

Truss, L. (2003) *Eats, Shoots and Leaves: The Zero Tolerance Approach to Punctuation*. London: Profile Books.

Turabian, Kate L. (2013) *A Manual for Writers of Research Papers, Theses, and Dissertations*. 8th edn. Chicago: Chicago University Press.

Ward, Lesley J. and Woods, Geraldine (2007) *English Grammar for Dummies*®. UK edn. Chichester: Wiley.

White, Eileen (2000) 'The Domestic Scene'. In: Eileen White (ed.), *Feeding a City: York – The Provision of Food from Roman Times to the Beginning of the Twentieth Century*. Totnes, Devon: Prospect Books.

# INDEX